SpringerBriefs in Economics

SpringerBriefs present concise summaries of cutting-edge research and practical applications across a wide spectrum of fields. Featuring compact volumes of 50 to 125 pages, the series covers a range of content from professional to academic. Typical topics might include:

- A timely report of state-of-the art analytical techniques
- A bridge between new research results, as published in journal articles, and a contextual literature review
- A snapshot of a hot or emerging topic
- An in-depth case study or clinical example
- A presentation of core concepts that students must understand in order to make independent contributions

SpringerBriefs in Economics showcase emerging theory, empirical research, and practical application in microeconomics, macroeconomics, economic policy, public finance, econometrics, regional science, and related fields, from a global author community.
Briefs are characterized by fast, global electronic dissemination, standard publishing contracts, standardized manuscript preparation and formatting guidelines, and expedited production schedules.

More information about this series at https://link.springer.com/bookseries/8876

Ligita Gasparėnienė • Rita Remeikienė
Colin C. Williams

Unemployment and the Informal Economy

Lessons From a Study of Lithuania

Springer

Ligita Gasparėnienė
Vilnius University
Law faculty
Vilnius, Lithuania

Rita Remeikienė
Vilnius University
Law faculty
Vilnius, Lithuania

Colin C. Williams
Management School
University of Sheffield
Sheffield, UK

ISSN 2191-5504 ISSN 2191-5512 (electronic)
SpringerBriefs in Economics
ISBN 978-3-030-96686-7 ISBN 978-3-030-96687-4 (eBook)
https://doi.org/10.1007/978-3-030-96687-4

This Springer imprint is published by the registered company Springer Nature Switzerland AG
The registered company address is: Gewerbestrasse 11, 6330 Cham, Switzerland

Acknowledgments

Funding for this work was provided by the Lithuanian Research Council under Grant [S-GEV-20-3].

Contents

Chapter 1
Introduction

What is the relationship between unemployment and the informal economy? Are those who engage in the informal economy exclusively those excluded from the formal labor market? And do they engage in informal work out of necessity due to the absence of alternative means of livelihood? The aim of this book is to answer these questions.

To do so, this book evaluates the relationship between the informal labor market and unemployment rate in the Republic of Lithuania, situated in the Northern European region. As noted by Černiauskas and Dobravolskas (2011), the Republic of Lithuania declared its independence from the Soviet Union in 1990, and immediately took on the work of simultaneously building a nation state and implementing the market reforms focused on price liberalization and small-scale privatization. Like most other post-Soviet transition economies, the informal economy has remained an extensive and persistent feature of the Lithuanian economy. According to Medina and Schneider's (2018) estimations, the size of the informal economy in Lithuania in 2017 was 23.8% of GDP, which significantly exceeded the European Union (EU) average of 16.6% of GDP. Thus, Lithuania still faces economic problems, such as large informal economies, akin to transition, and emerging economies. Based on ILO data (ILO, 2021), the average size of the informal economy in Lithuania in 1991–2015 period amounted to 25.2% of GDP.

Turning to the relationship between the informal economy and unemployment, there are many assumptions but until now little evidence. In other words, there are strong assertions but scant data. Until now, researchers have used econometric models to investigate the relationship between the unemployment rate and the informal economy at the national level (Alexandru et al., 2010; Sahnoun & Abdennadher, 2019; Dell'Anno & Solomon, 2008; Dobre & Alexandru, 2009; Bajada & Schneider, 2009). However, the literature is not rich in studies that reveal why this relationship is positive or negative. Even a cursory review of the literature indicates a lack of research on the relationship between the unemployment rate and the informal economy and even less research has been undertaken on what needs to be done in terms

L. Gasparėnienė et al., *Unemployment and the Informal Economy*, SpringerBriefs in Economics, https://doi.org/10.1007/978-3-030-96687-4_1

of policy approaches. Until now, the unemployment rate in the EU member states (including Lithuania) is mainly managed by invoking active labor market policy measures and employment promotion programs.

This book, however, adopts a rather different conceptualization of unemployment and approach towards tackling this phenomenon based on a recognition of the existence of the informal economy. To do so, first, it reveals the reasons for the reluctance/refusal of the unemployed to renounce their unemployment status; second, it discloses the proportion of the officially registered unemployed who are unemployed voluntarily due to their involvement in informal economic activities (acting as suppliers or sellers) and what causes of their involvement in the informal economy are most significant; third, it indicates what proportion of the unemployed tend to use services/buy goods in the informal sector due to their poor financial situation and what consequences this behavior has for the economy. In doing so, this book provides one of the first nuanced and richer understandings of the relationship between unemployment and the informal economy, the impacts of this relationship on formal economies, and how this problem can be tackled. The outcome will be to advance understandings of the informal economy by not only developing theoretical explanations of the relationship between the informal economy and unemployment but also how this can be tackled. This will fill a major and important gap in understandings about who engages in the informal economy and why they do so, as well as how it can be addressed in policy.

1.1 Setting the Scene

The informal sector is a significant part of the economy and the labor market across the globe. Indeed, 61% of the global labor force have their main employment in the informal economy. However, the informal economy is more prevalent in some economies than others. As the ILO (2015) find, in economies that are characterized by high rates of population growth and lower levels of GDP per capita, the informal sector tends to absorb the unemployed and surplus labor from the formal sector during periods of economic downturn and crises. Informal work can be either a strategy for survival for the unemployed, which is more the case in developing economies, or an attractive way to realize one's abilities and pursue independent activities, which is more the case in developed economies.

According to Slonimczyk (2014), in developing and transition economies, some half of the labor force works in the informal sector and uses public infrastructure and public services, but does not contribute to the infrastructure building, development or public service funding through paying taxes. This is also the case in the developed world. The current situation in labor markets across the world is severely affected not only by the remains of the global economic crisis of 2008–2009, but also by the consequences of the crisis caused by the COVID-19 pandemic. In such a volatile economic context, observed over the last decade or so, national labor markets have deeply deteriorated. According to the statistics provided by Eurostat

(2021) on the European Union, 15.278 million men and women in the 27 member states of the European Union (EU-27) were unemployed in May 2021. Compared with May 2020, the number of persons unemployed rose by 949,000. This is likely to have led to the enlargement of the informal sector. This has had severe impacts on the working conditions and living standards of those who participate. Although, on one hand, economic agents operating in the informal sector can earn some income for living and in an ideal case even realize their entrepreneurial potential, on the other hand, they are not entitled to social protection, unemployment benefits, illness, paternity or maternity, disability, and other benefits and social services, which makes them socially vulnerable.

The problem of the high unemployment rate calls for the development of the measures that would promote population's involvement into the labor market. One of the main aims defined in the Europe 2020 strategy is to have 75% of the active population (aged from 20 to 64) formally employed (European Commission, 2010). To achieve this, however, requires that informal work is transformed into formal work (ILO, 2015). Unless this is achieved, it seems unlikely that it will be possible to raise employment participation rates in the formal economy. Indeed, when it is recognized that a proportion of those operating in the informal economy do so out of choice, due to their desire to exit the formal economy (Lehmann & Pignatti, 2018; Srija & Shirke, 2014), it becomes obvious that participation in the informal economy is not simply some necessity-driven endeavor resulting from the exclusion of groups from the formal economy but is often a voluntary choice resulting from formal institutional failings that lead workers to exit the formal economy.

This book examines the dynamics between the informal economy and unemployment rates, the causes of informality, its consequences and potential reduction measures at both the theoretical and empirical levels. Reviewing what has been previously written, the arguments are so different that they provide no consensus on the relationship or the optimal measures to reduce the size of the above-mentioned phenomenon. Temkin (2009) notes that due to the heterogeneity and multiple dimensions inherent in the entire informal sector, even definitions of the informal economy and unemployment are not universal, but depend on the author's interpretation, their research purpose, the relationship between the factors under consideration, etc. This book seeks to review these previous studies and to bring some coherence to understanding the relationship between unemployment and participation in the informal economy.

1.2 Why Lithuania?

The relationship between the unemployment rate and the informal economy has been subject to much discussion. Until now, however, there have been few empirical studies which provide a nuanced understanding of this relationship. The assumption is that participation in the informal economy is largely by the unemployed in emerging economies. This book tests this thesis by examining Lithuania, a country that, based on the World Bank's classification, belongs to the group of emerging economies.

The theories of the informal economy propose that the relationship between unemployment rate and the informal economy can be positive (Okun's law), negative (the informal economy is growing in parallel with the formal economy), or non-existent (the phenomena are not interrelated).

To test this, this book reports an extensive survey conducted of participants in the informal economy in Lithuania. Until now, few if any studies have focused upon the relationship between the informal economy and unemployment. This paper fills that lacuna. This study focuses upon the relationship between unemployment and the informal economy, especially at the municipal level, in Lithuania. Based on 2019 data of the National Employment Service, the number of the unemployed in Lithuania has not been declining for several years and amounts to circa 143,000 unemployed; in other words, the economic growth and rising wages have not led to a decrease in the unemployment rate. The informal economy, meanwhile, is so far asserted in Lithuania to be largely determined by the population's financial situation in that citizens justify their engagement in informal activities according to their financial status (Lithuanian Free Market Institute, 2019). For example, if a person is satisfied with their income (in this case unemployment benefits), a person is 39% less likely to buy informal goods or services. Until now, however, no studies have been conducted on the extent to which the unemployed in Lithuania participate in the informal economy (from either a consumer's or a supplier's position), like elsewhere in the world. This book will fill that gap by reporting one of the first known in-depth studies of the relationship between unemployment and the informal economy.

1.3 Aims and Scope

The primary purpose of this book is to evaluate the interrelationship between the unemployment rate and the informal economy in Lithuanian municipalities. To achieve this, the book seeks to fulfill the following objectives:

1. To review the conceptual issues related to the informal sector and operation in the informal labor market.
2. To provide a profile of an economic agent acting in the informal labor market.
3. To conduct a comparative analysis of the general, rural, and urban-specific determinants of informality.
4. To classify the most common forms of informal employment.
5. To review the findings of previous studies concerning the nature of the relationship between unemployment and the informal economy.
6. To present the comparative analysis of the results obtained through the survey and the expert evaluation.

7. To provide an in-depth nuanced understanding of the dynamics between the unemployment rate and the informal economy.
8. To provide policy recommendations for addressing this issue.

1.4 The Structure

The book consists of four chapters: an introduction, theoretical part, empirical results, and conclusions and recommendations. This chapter explains the contents of the book and outlines its aims and scope. Chapter 2 then provides a comprehensive literature review of previous research on the informal economy, especially with regard to the relationship between unemployment and the informal economy. This is composed of six sections. Section 2.1, entitled "Conceptual issues of informal employment," reviews the concept of the informal economy in general, and the concept of informal employment more particularly, and reviews the main features of informality (unregistered activities or partial registration, tax evasion or partially paid taxes) and types of informal work (the informal self-employed, unofficially operating workers or households, permanent workers deprived of social security guarantees provided by an employer, agents operating with business licenses not offering employment contracts, etc.) in the informal market. Section 2.2, entitled "Profile of an agent acting in the informal labor market," then reviews what is so far known about the major characteristics of an agent operating in the informal labor market, such as their income, occupation, raw material and capital factors, expected benefits, demographic characteristics, education, place of residence, gender, age, marital status, social status, ethnicity, personal (ego) characteristics, personal abilities and skills, experience, factors of personal psychology, and tax morale. The general profile of an agent operating in the informal labor market covers a set of economic, demographic, and personal (ego) characteristics that reflect an agent's socioeconomic status, personality, and environment. The section also discusses the reasons for engaging in informal activities from the positions of exclusion-driven and opportunity-driven informal operators. Section 2.3, entitled "The causes of informality," addresses the different causes of informal employment in urban and rural areas. In the rural context, distrust in public authorities is greatest in areas where the population suffers from income inequality and limited access to resources. In the urban context, informality may be further exacerbated by problems related to the lack of social housing programs and insufficient public investment in urban infrastructure. In the rural context, informality is strongly affected by high economic (income) inequality, low level of human capital and close social ties in communities. The growth of the informal urban sector is driven by the soaring urban population, the rural–urban income gap, rural–urban migration and a large proportion of the poor. In addition, a significant role in rural areas is played by accessibility of credits because credits not only fund the start-up or restructuring of formal activities, but also facilitate economic transactions. Urban informality can be caused by poor financing infrastructures and the political decisions limiting participation of the private sector (financial institutions, savings and credit cooperatives, real estate developers, etc.). Section 2.4, entitled "Classification of the most common forms of informal employment," reviews the major forms of informal employment using various criteria, while Sect. 2.5, entitled "Informal employment and quality of life," analyses the links between informal employment and the quality of life. Finally, Sect. 2.6, entitled "The nature of the relationship between unemployment and the informal economy," reviews the potential natures of the relationship between unemployment rate and the informal economy. Although a positive relationship is most common, there are cases when empirical studies provide evidence of a negative or neutral relationship. To explain the latter types of relationship between unemployment and the informal economy, this chapter concludes by arguing that more comprehensive research is needed and thus displays why the research reported in this book has been undertaken.

Chapter 3 then reports one of the first known surveys to evaluate the relationship between the informal economy and unemployment, conducted in Lithuania. To do so, firstly, a description of the research methodology is provided, and secondly, an analysis of the empirical results. This is then followed in the fourth and final chapters by a concluding discussion of the findings and recommendations regarding both the theorization of this relationship as well as the policy implications, along with the limitations of the research and avenues for future research on this important topic.

Chapter 2
Theorizing the Informal Economy

2.1 Conceptualizing the Informal Economy

Historical and economic studies indicate that people in all societies have long adapted their activities to the regulations of their contemporary economic system either not to violate these regulations or to avoid them. Thus, if we treat informal economic activities as the activities that are conducted by evading the regulatory norms established in a regulated economic system, then we can state that the informal economy is the same age as the formal economy because implementation of regulated economic systems in societies worldwide provides an incentive for members of a society to circumvent the regulations, especially if they appear too strict, unjustified, or unfair.

Due to the informal economy being a complex, multi-faceted, and difficult-to-measure phenomenon, it is hard to define it precisely. As is noted by Habib-Mintz (2009), the concept of the informal economy is rather vague, as at different moments in history it has encompassed different paradigms, disciplines, and different interests, so its meaning has changed and evolved. For this reason, the literature on this phenomenon provides many different definitions of the informal (also referred to as the "hidden," "cash in hand," "shadow," "subterranean," "gray," "undeclared," "underground," "black," "unregulated," or "unaccounted") economy.

We will first present the general concepts of ***the informal economy*** that are found in the academic literature. Being a multifaceted phenomenon, the informal economy is defined by different authors according to what dimension, aspect or feature is their research focus. The most common definitions of the informal economy can be categorized as *fiscal, market (economic), legal,* and *statistical* (Brief Methodological Analyses, 2012). The basic context and features of the informal economy highlighted in the above-mentioned definitional categories are reviewed in Table 2.1.

L. Gasparėnienė et al., *Unemployment and the Informal Economy*, SpringerBriefs in Economics, https://doi.org/10.1007/978-3-030-96687-4_2

Table 2.1 Basic context and features of the informal economy highlighted in particular definitional categories

Basic context	Features	Author(s), year
Fiscal definitions		
The concepts of the informal economy are linked to the state budget damages	Tax evasion	Dell'Anno and Solomon (2008), Petersen et al. (2010), Schneider et al. (2010), Putninš and Sauka (2011), Reimers (2014), Medina and Schneider (2018), Enste (2018), Awasthi and Engelschalk (2018), Nchor (2021)
	Fraudulent financial payments	Petersen et al. (2010), Pickhardt and Prinz (2012), Gottschalk and Gunnesdal (2018)
	False accounting	Schneider et al. (2010), Putninš and Sauka (2011), Maftei (2013)
	Abuse of state benefits	Schneider and Enste (2002), Remeikiene et al. (2018)
Market (economic) definitions		
The concepts of the informal economy delve into the aspects of economic agents' operational performance	Work outside the formal labor market	Hope (2014), Loayza (2016), Enste (2018), Lambert et al. (2020)
	Activities to avoid strict market regulation	Petkantchin (2013), Manes et al. (2016), Enste (2018), Medina and Schneider (2018)
	Activities to reduce market entry and operating costs	Krstic and Radulovic (2015), Lithuanian Free Market Institute (2019)
	Competition distortions	Amaral and Quintin (2006), Leal-Ordonez (2013)
Legal definitions		
The concepts of the informal economy delve into the aspects of legal provision violations	Legally sanctioned (non-criminal) activities	Portes et al. (1989), Herwartz et al. (2013), Williams and Horodnic (2015a), Remeikiene et al. (2018)
	Non-compliance with legal standards	Schneider (2012), Lithuanian Free Market Institute (2015, 2019)
	Weakening socio-economic basis of collective agreements	Putninš and Sauka (2011)
	Poor protection of economic agents by the state	Hope (2014), Arsic et al. (2015)
Statistical definitions		
The concepts of the informal economy are linked to non-declaring and non-accounting aspects of an economic activity	Avoidance of providing statistical data, underreporting	Schneider et al. (2010), Herwartz et al. (2013), Ekici and Besim (2014), Putninš and Sauka (2015), Putninš et al. (2018)
	Exclusion from national income accounts (GDP distortions)	Mahmood (2020), Almenar et al. (2020)

Source: compiled by the authors

The information in Table 2.1 reveals that *fiscal definitions* of the informal economy tend to highlight features of this informality such as tax (income, value added, social security contributions, health insurance contributions, etc.) evasion, fraudulent financial payments, and settlements, false accounting (e.g., declaration of the minimum wage instead of the actual wage paid; so-called envelope wages), working time accounting frauds, etc. In the *market* (economic) definitions, the informal economy is defined more in terms of its characteristics such as work in the informal labor market, the conduct of unregistered activities to avoid strict market regulations and/or reducing market entry and operating costs, and the malpractices of economic operators whereby they compete unfairly with operators in the formal market, thereby distorting market competition principles. In the *legal* definitions, the informal economy is defined as exchanges of legal products and services (i.e., non-criminal) that nevertheless are exchanged in a manner that violates tax, social security, and labor laws (e.g., occupational safety requirements, established administrative procedures), and thus weaken the socio-economic basis of collective agreements and exclude informal operators from a state's legal protection system (e.g. informal operators cannot sue the other party for non-performance of contractual obligations). In the *statistical* definitions, fourth and finally, the informal economy is defined as the non-participation of informally active economic operators in statistical data collection and accounting systems (i.e., informal operators do not provide any or comprehensive data on their activities to the statistical authorities, state tax authorities, labor inspectorates, and so forth) and the exclusion of these data from national income accounts, which leads to distortions in GDP calculations.

If the nature of an activity differs in any way other than those outlined in the definitions reviewed above, then it is not defined as the informal economy. For instance, trafficking in illegal goods (arms, drugs, etc.) is not considered a part of the informal economy, but a part of the wider criminal economy (Rei, 2018; Remeikiene et al., 2018; Medina & Schneider, 2018; Bonnet et al., 2019b, etc.). In other words, where the products and services provided are illegal, they are not part of the informal economy. Instead, they are part of the broader criminal economy. Indeed, the so-called shadow economy often refers to both activities in the informal economy and these wider criminal activities, which explains why the calculations of its size are so much higher than calculations of the size of the informal economy. Moreover, it needs to be recognized that the informal economy only refers to paid work. If the activity is unpaid, it is treated as part of the unpaid economy (e.g., Pichio, 2003; Williams & Horodnic, 2015a; PWC, 2017).

Apart from the definition of the informal economy, another important hotly debated and discussed issue in the literature on this topic is its macroeconomic impact. Ulyssea (2018) and Lambert et al. (2020) note that the macroeconomic impact of the informal sector is not evident *ex ante*, but it is significant in terms of both its positive and negative impacts. This is interesting because much of the literature, especially that using fiscal, legal, and statistical definitions, tends to focus upon only its negative impacts.

In a positive sense, the informal sector provides economic agents with a sufficiently high degree of operational flexibility, which can serve to promote real economic growth, especially if the regulatory framework is extremely strict and restrictive. This is confirmed by Leyva and Urrutia's (2020) research which reveals that the informal sector raises resilience of the economy by helping to absorb internal and external shocks. On the other hand, others assert that an enlarged informal sector can limit economic growth through some other channels, such as by limiting the provision of public goods (Gerxhani, 2004; ILO, 2016), distorted resource allocation and distorted business decisions in the informal sector; by acting informally, business enterprises cannot expand freely (Ulyssea, 2018).

According to Lambert et al. (2020), the level of informality will always be relatively high because the demand for formal goods is insufficient, meaning that the demand for goods and services in the informal sector continues to be relatively high. Stuart et al. (2018) note that this demand for products and services from the informal economy is increasing with the growing demand for personal and household services. In addition, businesses operating in the formal and informal sectors of the economy bear different costs of market entry, employee retention and wages; thus, acting in the informal sector can help businesses reduce operational costs. Meanwhile, Lambert et al. (2020) also argue that the informal sector limits economic growth through the limitations of the consumer sector—goods and services produced in the informal sector are typically consumed by domestic consumers (households), while goods produced in the formal sector can be exported and consumed by a wider range of purchasers. The negative impact of the narrowness of the demand channel, inherent to the informal sector, on economic growth is also emphasized by La Porta and Shleifer (2014). These authors argue that since the share of goods and services produced in the informal sector and consumed by domestic consumers (households) is relatively small, business revenues from informal activities are also relatively small and may be insufficient either to cover fixed costs or to expand and modernize a business. These results are in line with Leyva and Urrutia's (2020) findings which propose that the informal sector leads to excessive output volatility. The above arguments suggest that the relationship between the informal economy and GDP per capita is decreasing and concave (Lambert et al., 2020).

Colombo et al. (2019) also envisage both positive and negative macroeconomic impacts of the informal sector. They note that the informal sector acts as a buffer zone mitigating the effects of economic crises that "absorbs" the surplus labor of the unemployed during crises. Some studies (National Planning Commission, 2012; Schneider et al., 2015) indicate that the activities of the unemployed in the informal economy are a natural part of an economic cycle because the informal sector absorbs surplus labor from the formal sector during periods of economic downturn. The close relationship between the informal economy and the labor market is confirmed by Perry et al. (2007), Fialova (2010), Pocius (2015), and many other authors. Nevertheless, Rogan and Skinner's (2017) and Burger and Fourie's (2019) do not confirm the potential of the informal sector to absorb surplus labor.

At the same time, the informal sector can act to reinforce further the impacts of a crisis. Under the conditions of a financial shock that accompanies an economic crisis, the formal economy is shrinking significantly, and the deeper and longer lasting is the crisis, the greater is the expansion of the informal sector. An enlarged informal sector involves many more informally employed, and thus diminishes the official formal employment participation rate. This is confirmed by the empirical results. In an empirical study based on the DSGE model, Colombo et al. (2019) found that deeper financial crises in developing economies lead to a greater redistribution of resources to less efficient sectors of the economy, with a larger share of the population experiencing the negative effects of informality.

On balance, it can be concluded that current literature does not provide any universal definition of the informal economy. The phenomenon under consideration can be conceptualized in several different ways and is defined depending on a selected research purpose to highlight the features of this complex economic phenomenon relevant to a particular study being conducted. In general, nevertheless, there is consensus regarding the type of economic activity that falls under the umbrella of this term. The informal economy can be defined as any activity that is not recognized, registered, protected, or/or regulated by the public authorities when it should be so. It is important to note. Moreover, that studies separate the concept of the informal economy from illegal, or criminal, activity and the unpaid economy because the former involves illegal products and services, and the latter does not generate revenue for an economic agent, while the informal economy is neither criminal nor unpaid, but is deliberately concealed from the authorities to evade tax, social security, and/or labor law.

Meanwhile, the macroeconomic impact of the informal sector is not obvious ex ante, but it is significant in terms of both potential positive and negative impacts. The positive macroeconomic impact of the informal sector is manifested in business flexibility, reduction of operating costs, and absorption of internal and external economic and financial shocks. The negative macroeconomic impact of the informal sector is manifested in a resultant shortage of public goods, distorted resource allocation, distorted business decisions in the informal sector, limited business development potential, narrowness of the demand channel, excessive output volatility and a crisis boosting effect, diminishing the official market participation rate.

Employment in the informal economy is, however, a slightly narrower concept compared to the concept of the informal economy. The above-presented literature suggests that the relationship between the informal economy and the unemployment rate manifests itself as the ability of the informal economy to absorb the surplus unemployment during an economic crisis; apart from that, it also possesses the potential to deepen a crisis by diminishing the official market participation rate. Hence, in this context, we need to narrow the general concept of the informal economy and link it to the informal labor market and the informal income-generating activities conducted by economic agents (both workers and the self-employed) that are not declared to the authorities for tax, social security, and/or labor law purposes (OECD, 2012; Schneider & Williams, 2013; Williams & Horodnic, 2015a), i.e. to the concepts of labor market informality, employment in the informal sector, informal employment or informal wage employment and informal self-employment. Nevertheless, even in this narrower context, informality in the labor market is difficult to define because it is characterized by several dimensions, legal aspects and the varying nature of both the labor market itself and the current and potential occupations.

Labor market informality. This is often unjustifiably associated with the developing world. For example, according to data provided by Loayza (2016), in a typical developing economy, as much as 35% of GDP is generated in the informal sector which employs about 70% of a country's workforce. However, the concept of the informal labor market is much more widely relevant because labor market informality is also observed in developed economies. In fact, the informal labor market involves the agents representing different activity areas. Although the literature does not provide any universal definition of the informal labor market, the general view considers economic agents (individuals) and their employers who engage in productive or service provision activities that are not officially registered and are conducted without paying taxes. The definition of labor market informality, provided by Lambert et al. (2020), emphasizes the aspect of non-compliance with legal norms; the authors treat labor market informality as activities conducted by economic agents outside the legal norms and regulations established in the country. They are of the opinion that in the context of non-compliance with legal provisions, the problem of labor market informality arises when the above-mentioned legal regulations are only established for being established (i.e., they serve their own purpose, but are not aimed at a specific regulatory objective and are, therefore, incapable of meeting the interests of economic operators). This means that economic agents prefer operating in the informal labor market because they feel that their interests or even their rights are not protected when they operate in the formal sector, and the conditions for their economic activities are unacceptable.

Nevertheless, the concept of labor market informality, based solely on such a legalistic approach, is considered too broad. As early as 1989, Hernando De Soto observed that the line between formal and informal activities is very difficult to draw following solely a legalistic approach because in specific cases, the features of complying with one provision, but not complying with another can be envisaged (De Soto, 1989). Therefore, even in a legal context, it should be clarified which specific provisions are infringed when conducting informal activities. Namely, whether it is laws relating to the conduct of an economic activity when an individual economic agent acts informally that are being infringed, whether it is laws relating to the accrual and payment of wages when an economic operator has unregistered employees, or whether it is laws relating to the obligation to pay social insurance contributions when this obligation is not fulfilled. Or even whether it is workers' health and occupational safety laws that are being infringed. It is also important to understand the degree of compliance with other legal provisions is observed (Kanbur, 2009). Put another way, there is a need to understand the degree of formalization or informalization. Businesses and workers are commonly not either fully informal or fully formal. Rather, they display a degree of in/formalization.

Another approach that defines informality in the labor market is the productivity approach. In this approach, informality in the labor market is perceived through the prism of job characteristics (Perry et al., 2007; Khamis, 2009). In this context, labor market informality is commonly linked to the informal operation of unskilled or low-skilled economic agents (e.g., non-professionals), marginal jobs, underground activities of the self-employed, and small firms with up to five workers, and domestic and family workers (Hussmanns, 2004; Khamis, 2009). With reference to the International Labor Organization (2002), the informal labor market is characterized by small-scale productive units with a low level of organization, weak labor-capital division, and casual employment, kinship or personal and communal tie-based labor relations (formal labor contracts are not established).

As is noted by Khamis (2009), the two above-described approaches to labor market informality – legalistic and productivity approaches – may overlap, but at the same time they differ from each other in that they may cover both the aspects of legal regulation infringements and the aspects of involvement of different economic operators. This reveals the heterogeneity inherent in the informal labor market.

Since in economic terms, the informal sector involves both individuals and their start-up or established production units through which informal activities are conducted, some authors invoke the concept of ***employment in the informal sector***. This is defined both in terms of characteristics inherent to production units (the enterprise approach) and characteristics inherent to economic agents involved in the informal sector (the labor approach) (Hussmanns, 2004). The definition adopted at the Fifteenth International Conference of Labor Statisticians (15th ICLS) (ILO, 2003), which took place in January 1993, is based on the former approach and considers enterprises operating in the informal sector to be owned by either individuals or households whose activities are not financially separated from their enterprise activities. It should be noted that the enterprise-based definition, provided by the 15th ICLS, is relevant to the purposes of recording labor statistics and national accounts, but it does not reflect all aspects of employment informalization, in particular with regard to characteristics of economic agents involved.

Srija and Shirke (2014) cite the definition, provided by the National Commission for Enterprises in the Unorganized Sector (NCEUS); the definition is based on the second labor-based approach, and reflects which economic agents participate in the informal labor market. This definition proposes that employment in the informal sector covers the informal workers or households but excludes regular workers who work with social security guarantees provided by employers, and the workers that operate in the formal sector without any social security guarantees provided by employers. In contrast to the former case, this latter approach does not consider participation of informally operating enterprises but focuses on participation of individuals and households. In addition, it does not recognize that economic agents operating in the informal sector can also have a formal job (i.e., to conduct an informal activity as a secondary one) or a status of formal employment. The definition provided by Hussmanns (2004) covers all the above-mentioned aspects and is, therefore, more comprehensive. Based on it, employment in the informal sector is referred to as "all jobs in informal sector enterprises or all persons who, during a given reference period, were employed in at least one informal sector enterprise, irrespective of their status in employment and whether it was their main or a secondary job" (p. 2). This definition considers participation of both enterprises and individuals and takes into account potential heterogeneity of the participants' status.

The topic under consideration is closely linked to the concept of ***informal employment*** or ***informal wage employment***. In a general sense, Srija and Shirke

(2014) conceptualize formal employment as organized, while informal employment is treated as unorganized. In a narrower sense, the concept of informal employment can be linked to an enterprise-based approach and a job-based approach, but in this case the characteristics of economic agents involved remain in the background. The definition, developed by the National Commission for Enterprises in the Unorganized Sector (NCEUS), proposes that informal (or unorganized) employment refers to the activities of "all unincorporated private enterprises owned by individuals or households engaged in the sale and production of goods and services operated on a proprietary or partnership basis and with less than ten workers" (cited by Srija & Shirke, 2014, p. 40). The latter definition highlights disorganization of informal work and the potential forms of informal activities, but it does not provide the basis on which the maximum number of workers involved is set.

In the context of the potential forms of informal activities, informal employment is defined by the ILO as "the total number of informal jobs, whether carried out in formal sector enterprises, informal sector enterprises, or households, during a given reference period" (the definition provided by the 17th ICLS, cited by Hussmanns (2004), p. 5). Considering the role of economic agents, it should be noted that this definition assumes that economic agents can perform both formal and informal work simultaneously, but concerning the subject, it focuses on the conduct of activities through production units (i.e. enterprises, households) and does not consider the activities of own-account workers (when economic agents act not through micro-enterprises, but as individuals) that make a statistically significant share of informal employment. For instance, Rutkowski's (2011) empirical findings suggest that around half of all workers in the informal sector are own-account workers. Based on the ILO statistical data provided by Bonnet et al. (2019a), the share of own-account workers in developed countries in 2016 accounted for 67.2% of total informal employment excluding the agricultural sector, and 68.8% of total informal employment including the agricultural sector. Nevertheless, this definition is seen as explaining informal unemployment not only in developing but also in developed economies because namely enterprises here are treated as economic units that respond to competitive pressures forcing them to undertake informal or mixed-mode labor arrangements that comprise a variety of non-standard, alternative, irregular, and other forms of subcontracting (Hussmanns, 2004). Meanwhile, an individual forced by competitive pressures may make other decisions (e.g., register as unemployed, live on unemployment benefits provided by the state). In the latter case, an individual is no longer a participant in the informal labor market.

The International Labor Organization (2002) explains informal waged employment as a form of work where employees work in informal or formal enterprises. Hussmanns (2004) notes in this context that the term "enterprise" refers to any unit that is engaged in production of goods or provision of services for sale or barter. Informal employment can therefore include informal employees working in formal enterprises for "envelope" wages, casual day workers, undeclared workers, part-time or temporary workers without formal labor contracts, street vendors, domestic workers, home workers and the self-employed (both individuals and households) that conduct economic activities independently and have no formal employer. The latter can operate without setting up a company, set up a micro-enterprise, work alone or with family members, relatives, and have salaried employees. The activities can be conducted either inside or outside an economic agent's home, activity premises can be identifiable, unidentifiable or an activity may not have any fixed location.

In the last decade, studies have recognized the participation of the self-employed in the informal labor market as significant (Fiess et al., 2010; Neves et al., 2011; Adom, 2014; Williams & Horodnic, 2015b; Mussurov & Arabsheibani, 2015; Williams & Bezeredi, 2017; Ojong, 2017; Yu et al., 2020, etc.). This is why it is relevant to analyze the concept of ***informal self-employment***. According to the OECD (2008), self-employment can provide more opportunities for informal activities than being an informal employee, not least because detecting informal self-employment is very complicated but also because there exists more opportunities for informality amongst the self-employed than amongst waged employees in many countries. In addition, formal employees can operate informally as self-employed not only outside formal work hours, but also by subcontracting to the same employer, thus reducing their tax liability. The latter phenomenon is referred to as false self-employment and is relatively common in the central European countries (OECD, 2008).

Like most concepts of the informal economy and informal work, informal self-employment is defined in different ways, but the literature mainly focuses on two approaches: on one hand, informal self-employment is treated as a way for the poor to survive; on the other hand, it can be an attractive way to realize one's abilities and pursue independent activities. The difference between the above-mentioned interpretations is best reflected in the division of the informal self-employment sector proposed by Fields (1990). Informal self-employment is divided into a "lower tier" (reflecting the necessity-driven first approach) and an "upper tier" (reflecting the agency-oriented second approach). Williams (2007), Adom (2014), Williams and Youssef (2014), and Beyer and Morgan (2018) propose the concepts of necessity- and opportunity-driven self-employment, Perry et al. (2007), Williams and Youssef (2015), Williams and Bezeredi (2017) use the concepts of exclusion-driven and exit-driven informal self-employment, while Williams and Horodnic (2015b), Sauka et al. (2016), Stuart et al. (2018), and some others lean on the marginalization and reinforcement thesis, respectively.

The authors describing the first necessity-driven approach to depict informal self-employment note that such exclusion-driven self-employment is a residual phenomenon that stems from the incapability of the formal economy to absorb the unemployed (Temkin, 2009). Thus, the exclusion-driven self-employed are usually the ones who have lost their job temporarily or permanently, so operating in the informal sector is one of their few choices or even their only choice. Work in this sector is often deemed unpleasant and even degrading. The exclusion-driven self-employed are doomed to the trap of absolute poverty (Maloney, 2003; Temkin, 2009; Nygaard & Dreyer, 2020).

On the other hand, the second agency-oriented approach views informal self-employment more as a voluntary decision, and one taken out of choice rather than necessity. It is adopted as a choice rather than due to lack of choice. This approach tends to focus upon the informal self-employment as a form of entrepreneurship and emphasizes the entrepreneurial dynamism that attracts economic agents to freely choose to act as the informal self-employed. Keith Hart, who conducted a study in Kenya in 1972, emphasizes that it is the entrepreneurial spirit that stimulates economic agents' willingness to assume risks, manage their own activities, and exploit the human and capital resources available. In the latter case, informal self-employment stems from the developments in the formal sector, when economic agents under the competitive pressures try to reduce their operating costs and raise competitiveness. These individuals may also seek independence from employers, look forward to exploiting opportunities, and earning higher income (e.g., in the case of employment in a formal enterprise engaged in a similar activity, a part of the income goes to the employer). Exit-driven self-employed are often not only those who do not do any formal work, but also those who work directly or indirectly in formal enterprises. The work in this sector can be varied; an economic agent chooses it according to their abilities, aspirations, and the market demand. As noted by Williams and Horodnic (2015b), the exit-driven self-employed are usually affluent, educated, and sufficiently professional. In this respect, according to Temkin (2009), the exit-driven informal self-employment sector in developing economies is similar to the voluntary entrepreneurship sector in developed economies.

Although some researchers base their studies on the more conventional poverty trap approach (Ogunrinola, 2011; Dellot, 2012; Magidimisha & Gordon, 2015; Pfau-Effinger, 2017; Sahoo & Neog, 2017, etc.), an increasing number of studies (Maloney, 2003; Temkin, 2009; Gunther & Launov, 2012; Williams & Horodnic, 2015b; Williams & Bezeredi, 2017, etc.) analyze and compare both approaches and provide calculations of the ratio of the informally operating self-employed attributable to both categories. Nevertheless, the results of previous studies concerning which group of the informally operating self-employed - exclusion or exit-driven - is more abundant, are contradictory. For instance, Temkin's (2009) research revealed that the largest share of the respondents in the Mexican labor force are characterized by vulnerability, insecurity, and low education (i.e., the characteristics typical of the exclusion-driven self-employed). Gunther and Launov's (2012) research in developing countries discloses that the proportion who treat informal self-employment as an attractive employment opportunity is smaller than the proportion of those to whom informal self-employment is a strategy of last resort in the absence of alternative livelihoods. Williams and Horodnic (2015b), who analyzed the situation in 28 European countries, found that the marginalization approach applies in terms of the informal self-employed age, marital status, tax morality, occupation, and household finance determinants, but the reinforcement approach is valid in terms of their gender and regional variations. Meanwhile, Williams and Bezeredi's (2017) multinomial regression analysis of a representative sample of 1430 businesses in Bulgaria, Croatia, and FYR Macedonia revealed that for every exclusion-driven self-employed, there are three exit-driven self-employed (i.e., the number of the latter is three times higher). Thus, the real character of informal self-employment remains hard to decipher and may depend on the level of a country's economic development. In any case, the issue is complicated since the two above-mentioned scenarios practically always have very different meanings and implications related to the magnitude of distortions in the formal labor market.

Nevertheless, regardless of which of the two approaches is followed by particular studies and which proportion of the informal self-employed is found to represent either exclusion or opportunity category, some key features of informal self-employment can be singled out:

1. economic agents operating in the informal self-employment sector are socially unprotected and unrepresented by formal labor organizations or unions (Maloney, 2003);
2. the income of economic agents operating in the informal self-employment sector is characterized by volatility (ILO, 2002; Temkin, 2009, etc.), which makes this sector not completely secure financially;
3. the informal self-employment sector is characterized by lower rates of productivity growth (ILO, 2002) because acting informally, economic agents cannot expand their activities freely.

On balance, when researching the relationship between unemployment and the informal economy, we here employ the concept of labor market informality which is narrower than the general concept of the informal sector (i.e., in this study, informal activities in the labor market are treated as income-generating activities for informal workers or the self-employed). It should be noted that even within this limited approach, informal activities in the labor market are difficult to define because of their high degree of heterogeneity and inclusion of several different dimensions, primarily violations of legal regulations, job characteristics, economic agents' characteristics, the degree of market organization, the forms of informal activities, and the motives for involvement (the necessity to survive or a free will). Although the results of previous studies are contradictory in terms of estimating which group of the informal self-employed – exclusion or exit-driven – is predominant, literature analysis proposes that the essential features of informal self-employment are the lack of social security for economic agents, income volatility and lower rates of productivity growth.

Considering the significant macroeconomic impacts of the informal economy and informal labor market, it can be stated that a deeper analysis of the relationship between the two phenomena can help to improve the measures undertaken to reduce the unemployment rate and the labor market slack, and to better assess the impact of informality on the formal economy. In addition, it can contribute to developing the measures that would motivate those working in the informal sector at least in part, and ideally fully, to transfer their work to the formal sector.

2.2 Profile of an Agent Acting in the Informal Labor Market

Having discussed these conceptual issues, another important aspect is to identify which agents tend to operate in the informal economy. That is, to provide a profile of who is more likely to be an informally acting agent. As noted by Hjort and Lantz (2012), the differences in the behavior of agents can be caused not only by their desire to reduce operating costs, but also by certain demographic and personal characteristics such as their age, income, education, place of residence, and so forth. In a general sense, labor markets are not segmented but competitive, and the informal sector is formed because economic agents are characterized by heterogeneous abilities and priorities. In addition, as mentioned in the previous conceptual section, there are two approaches to individuals operating in the informal labor market. It is considered that some of them work informally because it is necessary for their survival and family upkeep, while others see it as a potential to earn higher income and operate an independent business. Thus, the profile of an economic agent operating in the informal labor market can be different, depending on their main motivation for participating in the informal economy.

Characteristics of economic agents operating in the informal labor market have been analyzed by Slavnic (2010), Arunatilake and Jayawardena (2010), Tefera and Delbiso (2013), Schneider and Williams (2013), Altbeker and Storme (2013), Taiwo (2013), Slonimczyk (2014), Williams et al. (2015), Sahoo and Neog (2017), Williams and Horodnic (2015b), Kolm and Larsen (2016), Williams et al. (2017), Ramasamy et al. (2017), Li et al. (2018), and many others. Based on an analysis of this literature, the major characteristics of exclusion-driven and opportunity-driven economic agents operating in the informal labor market are documented in Table 2.2.

The information in Table 2.2 indicates that a profile of economic agents operating in the informal labor market is mainly shaped by economic, demographic and personal (ego) characteristics.

In the category of **economic characteristics,** the most influential factors are an agent's income, occupation, raw materials and capital at their disposition, and expected benefits.

Income. A substantial literature proposes that low-income earners are more likely to engage in informal activities and operate in the informal labor market compared with higher income earners. It is noted that high-income earners do not possess one of the main motives – an economic motive – to engage in informal activities, so informal activities are commonly linked to low-income earners (Rosenbaum et al., 2011; Sirkeci & Magnusdottir, 2011; Lithuanian Free Market Institute, 2015, etc.). The reports provided by National Planning Commission (2012) and Schneider et al. (2015) suggest that the unemployed tend to engage in informal economic activities so as not to lose state-paid unemployment benefits, but at the same time they seek alternative sources of income, which also prove that the income of those operating in the informal labor market is not high. According to Nygaard and Dreyer (2020), those working in the informal sector are twice as likely as those working in the formal sector to belong to poor households. As noted by Burger and Fourie

Table 2.2 The major characteristics of exclusion-driven and opportunity-driven economic agents operating in the informal labor market

Characteristic categories	Exclusion-driven attitude	Opportunity-driven attitude	Author(s), year
Economic characteristics			
Income	Low-income earners, social benefit recipients from low-income households with a limited saving potential are more likely to engage in informal activities	Informal self-employed tend to have less financial difficulties and belong to more affluent population groups	Temkin (2009), Rosenbaum et al. (2011), National Planning Commission (2012), Sirkeci and Magnusdottir (2011), Lithuanian Free Market Institute (2015), Williams and Horodnic (2015b), Burger and Fourie (2019), Nygaard and Dreyer (2020)
Occupation	Low-skilled jobs, manual jobs	Crafts, sales, production, service provision; skilled and unskilled work; a type of occupation provides sufficient freedom for independent acting	Temkin (2009), Packard et al. (2012), Williams and Horodnic (2015b)
Raw material and capital factors	Lack of skills, capital, working premises, raw materials, adequate markets	Business start-up financing with own initial capital, working capital upkeeping from personal savings or by borrowing from an intermediary	Grimm et al. (2011), Brill (2011), Barbour and Llanes (2013), Tefera and Delbiso (2013), Slonimczyk (2014)
Expected benefits	Survival, family upkeep, improvement of standard of living	Improvement of standard of living, higher profits, self-positioning, non-monetary benefits	Maloney (2004), Fialova (2010), Tefera and Delbiso (2013)
Demographic characteristics			
Education	Lack of education and skills	Higher, college or manual education	Reimer and Bollman (2009a), Temkin (2009), Altbeker and Storme (2013), Slonimczyk (2014), Mussurov and Arabsheibani (2015), Kolm and Larsen (2016)

(continued)

Table 2.2 (continued)

Characteristic categories	Exclusion-driven attitude	Opportunity-driven attitude	Author(s), year
Place of residence	Third countries, poorer regions, peripheral rural areas, deprived urban neighborhoods	More affluent regions, urban areas	Reimer and Bollman (2009a), ILO (2012), Schneider and Williams (2013), Williams and (2014), Weng (2015), Kolm and Larsen (2016), Gadsby and Samson (2016), Simutina and Leventov (2018), Beyer and Morgan (2018)
Gender	In developing countries with a large part of population acting informally as exclusion-driven, female participation rate is higher than male	In developed countries with a greater potential of opportunity-driven informal employment, men are more likely to engage in informal activities	ILO (2002), Temkin (2009), Sirkeci and Magnusdottir (2011), Stoevska (2012), Packard et al. (2012), Amasiatu and Shah (2014), Magidimisha and Gordon (2015)
Age	In developing countries with a large part of population acting informally as exclusion-driven, older people are more likely to engage in informal employment	In developed countries with a greater potential of opportunity-driven informal employment, younger people (aged 15–24) are more likely to engage in informal activities compared to middle-aged or older people	Harris (2008), Sirkeci and Magnusdottir (2011), Chavdarova (2014)
Marital status	Divorced people, people with families and children	Separated, divorced and widowed people are more likely to engage in informal activities compared to single or married people	Maloney (2004), Temkin (2009), Amasiatu and Shah (2014), Williams and Horodnic (2015b)
Social status	Participation of people with a lower social status can be observed	Participation of people with a higher social status can be observed	Hsu and Shiue (2008), Temkin (2009), Slonimczyk (2014), Prelipcean et al. (2016)
Ethnicity	Ethnic minorities	Locals	Packard et al. (2012), Mussurov and Arabsheibani (2015)
Personal (ego) characteristics			
Personal abilities and skills	Lack of managerial abilities and skills, lack of specific skills	Managerial abilities and skills, specific abilities and skills,	Avirgan et al. (2005), Slonimczyk (2014)

(continued)

Table 2.2 (continued)

Characteristic categories	Exclusion-driven attitude	Opportunity-driven attitude	Author(s), year
Experience	Insufficient previous experience	Sufficient previous experience	Sinyavskaya and Popova (2005), Avirgan et al. (2005), Foscht et al. (2013)
Factors of personal psychology	Vulnerability in terms of a lack of self-confidence and low levels of subjective well-being, a lack of personal initiative, motivation and determination, creativeness, innovativeness, determination and persistence	Self-confidence, determination, persistence, independence, the need for achievement, internal locus of control, willingness and ability to assume risks, tolerance of uncertainty and ambiguity, and innovativeness	Mohar et al. (2007), Temkin (2009)
Tax morale	Individuals with lower tax morale	-	Williams and Horodnic (2015b)

Source: compiled by the authors

(2019), remuneration for work in the informal sector is commonly lower than that in the formal sector, though the former requires significantly lower skills than the latter. Low levels of income and education are also noted in the literature review provided by Temkin (2009). The empirical research conducted by Temkin (2009) revealed that compared with other labor market participants, the self-employed operating in the informal sector belong to a lower socio-economic stratum of society, are less satisfied with the financial and economic situation of their households and are not optimistic about their household saving potential. Nevertheless, Williams and Horodnic's (2015b) study reveals that the self-employed, who engage in the informal labor market for opportunity motives, tend to have fewer financial difficulties and belong to more affluent population groups compared with those whose operation in the informal labor market is exclusion driven. Williams and Bezeredi (2017) found that before entering the informal labor market, a substantial share of exit-driven self-employed were formally employed, retired or represented the category of the individuals without any significant financial difficulties.

Occupation. Regarding occupation, it should be noted that activities in the informal labor market are often conditioned by the individual freedom of action that can be provided by one or another occupation. Temkin (2009) argues that economic agents operating in the informal labor market often give priorities to informal trade and production because the latter can provide independence and initiative opportunities. Williams and Horodnic's (2015b) study revealed that crafts people and sellers have sufficient individual freedom to act as the informal self-employed, whereas this is not the case for prestigious professions such as doctors, lawyers or business proprietors whose main activities are carried out through institutions (in the above-mentioned cases, medical institutions, lawyers' offices, etc.) and who often belong to trade unions or chambers representing their interests.

On the other hand, Packard et al.'s (2012) analysis of the microdata representing the situation in Roma communities disclosed that exclusion-driven informal workers tend to be involved in manual and low-skilled jobs, while people who are informally self-employed are as likely to be doing skilled as unskilled work.

Raw material and capital factors. According to Grimm et al. (2011), individuals wishing to enter the informal sector may face barriers such as a lack of skills or capital. This opinion is supported by Brill (2011) and Barbour and Llanes (2013) who argue that the self-employed, more prone to operate in the informal sector, often face greater financial difficulties and/or belong to the group of low-income earners. Tefera and Delbiso (2013) additionally point to the barriers such as a lack of working premises, an adequate market and raw materials.

There are, however, opposing views. For instance, Slonimczyk (2014) notes that when operating in the informal sector as an opportunity-driven self-employed, an economic agent has to self-finance the business start-up and to provide working capital from personal savings or by borrowing from an intermediary (also often informally). And while entrepreneurs in the formal sector theoretically have access to more capital (bank loans, movable and immovable property, etc.), financing a business start-up and development with personal savings and personal loans is a faster and more flexible way of financing.

Expected benefits. If involvement of an economic agent in the informal labor market is exclusion-driven, then the major benefit expected from informal economic activities is earning a basic income for to survive (for food, clothing, housing, and other basic needs). The most important motive for families and those with children is family upkeeping (Maloney, 2004; Perry et al., 2007; Temkin, 2009, etc.). In rarer cases, exclusion-driven economic agents want to improve their standard of living. In any case, the expected benefits are purely economic. The inability to provide oneself with economic benefits by means other than informal activities is often associated with low levels of agents' education and a place of residence (e.g., poor rural areas).

Tefera and Delbiso's (2013) survey-based study, however, revealed that as many as 90% of the people working in the informal sector do so not because of low education or a place of residence, but because of an improvement of their standard of living. Tefera and Delbiso (2013) found that either higher education or city residence do not hinder agents' involvement in the informal sector due to wider opportunities to find a formal job, but, on the contrary, even provide them with higher profits and a longer stay in the informal sector. The profile of individuals seeking to position themselves in the informal sector due to the relatively large advantages and a relatively high profit potential is also confirmed in Maloney's (2004) study. Fialova (2010) additionally sees non-monetary benefits—personal satisfaction, freedom of activity, and self-realization.

In the category of demographic characteristics, the profile of an economic agent operating in the informal labor market mainly depends on an agent's education, place of residence, gender, age, marital status, social status, and ethnicity.

Education. Developed managerial or specific skills, often acquired through college or university education, are significant elements of the profile of an agent operating in the informal labor market in terms of opportunity-driven self-employment (Slonimczyk, 2014). Mussurov and Arabsheibani (2015) found that about half of the informal self-employed have secondary education, about one-third – technical/incomplete higher education, and 11–17% higher education (the figures do not differ much for male and female groups).

However, when analyzing the profile of an economic agent in terms of exclusion-driven informal self-employment, it should be noted that a significant role here is played by the lack of education and skills because this lack is a significant obstacle for the unemployed to find a job in the formal labor market. Altbeker and Storme (2013) provide the statistics, according to which the unemployment rate for early school leavers amounts to 50%. Kolm and Larsen (2016) state that informal work opportunities for manual workers or workers with low education are substantially higher than for those with higher education, especially in rural areas. According to Reimer and Bollman (2009a), residents of rural areas are not motivated to pursue knowledge and education because having access to only low-skilled jobs and facing the problems of a process complexity and high risks when trying to establish a business, they feel their efforts to raise skill levels will be wasted, and they will incur costs that will not pay off later.

On the other hand, Gerxhani and Werfhorst's (2011) research revealed that people with higher education are less likely to engage in informal activities. Gerxhani and Werfhorst (2011) argue that higher education means larger human capital – with the latter, an agent has more potential to earn higher income, so the incentives to operate in the informal sector are lower, primarily for financial reasons. Another aspect is that people with higher education are commonly characterized by higher moral principles and values and follow the norms of transparent civic activities. Based on the survey method, the authors found a strong negative relationship between education and individual participation in the informal sector.

There is also literature that does not provide evidence of the relationship between a person's education and participation in the informal labor market. For instance, Williams and Horodnic's (2015b) multilevel mixed-effects logistic regression analysis did not provide evidence that education is a significant determinant of either marginal (exclusion-driven) or opportunity-driven informal self-employment.

Place of residence. At the global regional level, Schneider and Williams (2013) identify that the likelihood of participation in the informal labor market is higher among residents of developing countries. The ILO's (2012) report expresses a similar position proposing that the informal self-employed are likely to reside in poorer regions of the global economy. When assessing the role of the place of residence at the local neighborhood level, many scholars (Brill, 2011; Dellot, 2012; Barbour & Llanes, 2013; Kolm & Larsen, 2016, etc.) are of the opinion that the informal self-employed are most likely to reside in peripheral rural areas or deprived urban neighborhoods. The modern knowledge-based economy, technological advancement, and globalization require a constant increase in the level of knowledge, but as noted by Gadsby and Samson (2016), rural communities do not even have a so-called learning culture. Based on the studies by Gadsby and Samson (2016), and Reimer and Bollman (2009a), a relationship between agents' participation in the informal economy and the place of residence can be envisaged: it was found that rural residents face more difficulties in finding a job than urban residents because with significantly lower investment flows (Ramasamy et al., 2017; Li et al., 2018) and a lack of infrastructure (Gadsby & Samson, 2016), regional residents are likely to face such relevant problems as a lack of attractive work places or work places in general (Williams, 2011), wage inequalities (Liu et al., 2011), and so forth. With reference to Weng (2015), the informal economy in rural areas is a source of livelihood for the poor, when the latter exploit natural resources (primarily land) to conduct economic activities, such as farming and timber production.

However, in the context of opportunity-driven informal self-employment, it should be noted that this type of informal activity, which as mentioned earlier can provide higher profits and higher standards of living, is more likely to require modern knowledge, practical, and technological skills, and mobility. It is therefore typical of urban residents and can be observed in more affluent regions (Krumplyte & Samulevicius, 2010; Williams, 2011; Williams & Youssef, 2014; Simutina & Leventov, 2018; Beyer & Morgan, 2018, etc.).

Nevertheless, the literature also contains studies that do not confirm the significant impact of the place of residence on the decision to operate in the informal market. For instance, Williams and Horodnic's (2015b) multilevel mixed-effects logistic regression analysis does not provide evidence that the urban-rural divide is a significant determinant of either marginal (exclusion-driven) or opportunity-driven informal self-employment.

Gender. Some studies provide evidence of the relationship between participation in the informal labor market and gender. For example, the sociodemographic data derived from the 2005 WVS in Mexico by Temkin (2009), as well as the studies conducted by Stanculescu (2005) in Eastern EU candidate countries and Bonnet et al. (2019b) in Southern Asia, Southern Africa, Latin America, and the Caribbean, find that women are more likely than men to be involved in the informal economy. Magidimisha and Gordon's (2015) in South Africa, a nation with a high unemployment rate, where the population is involved in informal self-employment to escape poverty, revealed that many South African women are currently informal self-employed. Men also enter the informal sector, and although they make up a minority, they tend to earn more than women.

The studies conducted by the ILO (2002), Sirkeci and Magnusdottir (2011), Stoevska (2012), and Amasiatu and Shah (2014), however, indicate that in developed economies men are more likely to engage in informal economic activities than women. Based on the ILO's (2002) statistical data, men are more commonly involved in informal activities than women, and this trend is observed in Eastern Europe (7 women for every 11 men), Western Europe (11 women for every 17 men), and other developed countries (9 women for every 12 men). The result of a higher participation rate in the informal economy for men was also provided by Stoevska (2012). These results are partly linked to the prevailing gender stereotypical thinking that a man's duty is to provide financial support for his family, so a man must have a job, whether formal or informal, to earn income for his family and ensure the family's well-being. Packard et al.'s (2012) research in Europe also confirms higher rates of male than female informal employment in most European countries, except for Romania where women make up the largest share of the waged informal labor force. Mussurov and Arabsheibani's (2015) findings suggest that the share of men and women in the informal economy is almost equal.

Age. In terms of relationship between participation in the informal labor market and age, the results of previous studies indicate that in developed countries, young people (aged 15–24) are more likely to participate in the informal labor market compared with middle-aged or older people (Harris, 2008; Sirkeci & Magnusdottir, 2011; Chavdarova, 2014). This trend is explained by the fact that developed countries have relatively high levels of youth unemployment. Based on the data provided by Statista (2021), the youth unemployment rate in the EU member states as of January 2021 varied from 18 to 39.9% (see Annex 1), which promotes young people to engage in the informal economy. As noted by Chavdarova (2014), the negative consequence is that these young people fall into an informality trap: initial work experience is very important when starting a job, and if participation in the economy starts with involvement in its informal side, then the chances of a person staying in a similar position lifelong are very high. Meanwhile, other authors who analyzed the situation in developing countries, where most of the population operating informally are exclusion-driven, found higher rates of participation among older age groups (Temkin, 2009; Packard et al., 2012). Williams and Horodnic's (2015b) study, however, revealed that this participation in the informal economy for necessity-driven reasons is more apparent among younger people.

Marital status. Although the literature is not rich in studies focused on the relationship between participation in the informal labor market and a person's marital status, some studies propose that this relationship can be significant. For instance, Amasiatu and Shah's (2014) research revealed that divorced, separated, or widowed people are more likely to operate in the informal sector than single or married people. In some societies, these hidden earnings from the informal economy enable those who are divorced to evade matrimony payments which would otherwise be incurred if they held formal declared sources of income. Williams and Horodnic (2015b) found that the widowed self-employed are more likely to participate in the informal economy for necessity-driven reasons. Given that the exclusion-driven self-employed treat informal activities as a source of income that would support their families and children, the studies conducted by Maloney (2004), Perry et al. (2007), and Temkin (2009) indirectly propose that the informally operating exclusion-driven self-employed are married with children.

Social status. Economic agents of lower social status are more likely to participate in the informal labor market than those of higher social status (Hsu & Shiue, 2008; Prelipcean et al., 2016). Hsu and Shiue (2008) found that individuals characterized by low social recognition (e.g., unattractive physical appearance, disrespectful occupation, previous criminal convictions) are more likely to engage in the informal economy. Temkin's (2009) empirical research disclosed that compared to other labor market participants, the self-employed operating in the informal sector belong to a lower socio-economic stratum of society. However, according to Slonimczyk (2014), the opportunity-driven informal self-employed are attributable to the middle and higher social classes because this status allows them to have bigger personal savings and more capital needed to start informal activities.

Ethnicity. Packard et al.'s (2012) study revealed that in EU member states, especially in the new ones, informally working individuals are predominantly both nationals rather than migrants and are also predominantly from the dominant rather than minority ethnic groups in their countries. However, in several countries those employed without a contract are more likely to be from native-born ethnic and linguistic minority groups (e.g., the Roma) who are a greater risk of exclusion from social protection and pathways out of poverty. The factor of ethnicity is also noted by Mussurov and Arabsheibani (2015) whose research on informal self-employment in Kazakhstan revealed a declining number of Kazakh and a rising number of ethnic minorities participating in informal self-employment.

In the category of **personal (ego) characteristics,** it is important to analyze the profile of an economic agent operating in the informal labor market in terms of their personal skills and abilities, previous experience, personal psychology, and tax morale.

Regarding ***personal skills and abilities***, the key components of an informal economic agent's profile are managerial abilities and skills, previous experience, specific abilities, and skills. Revealing the importance of managerial abilities and skills, Slonimczyk (2014) argues that individuals with greater managerial abilities tend to choose (in)formal self-employment, while individuals that possess less developed managerial abilities are inclined to select paid employment. Thus, the main assumption that can be applied to assess informal self-employment is that a person's managerial skills are a significant factor for conducting informal activities because this person is responsible for organizing and performing the activities selected (Slonimczyk, 2014).

Apart from managerial skills, the self-employed in the informal sector often possess some specific skills (Slonimczyk, 2014) which can be acquired through previous formal work or self-employment. For instance, individuals who have acquired the skills of a plumber or car mechanic in a previous job may choose to provide informal services in these occupations after their formal working hours or at weekends or start acting as the informal self-employed, especially if the expected economic benefits (the potential income from informal self-employment) are going to exceed the income from the formal work.

Different skills, either managerial or specific, develop and evolve through ***experience***. Thus, individuals operating in the informal labor market tend to have at least some prior experience. Avirgan et al. (2005) define experience as the number of *potential* years in the labor market. For example, Foscht et al. (2013) found that the positive previous experience in buying and /or selling goods informally (the authors analyzed the case of e-commerce) may push agents deeper into the informal economy.

A number of case studies reported by Avirgan et al. (2005) revealed that experience is a return-generating factor (the authors propose the term *"return on experience*"). Nevertheless, the results of a study of Egypt by El-Mahdi and Amer (2005) showed that a higher level of experience is typical of men and women operating in the formal rather than the informal sector of the economy. The authors found that the agents operating in the formal economy have an average of 20.3 years of potential experience, while those operating in the informal sector have an average of 14.3 years of potential experience. These results are in line with the findings of Sinyavskaya and Popova (2005) who identify how formal workers tend to have greater tenure and experience in comparison with informal workers.

Factors of personal psychology. Mohar et al. (2007) raise the idea that the informally operating self-employed have specific values as well as specific motivations for engaging in such endeavor. Based on Temkin's (2009) research, these agents are characterized by self-confidence, determination, persistence and self-reliance, the need for achievement, internal locus of control, willingness and ability to assume risks, tolerance of uncertainty and ambiguity, and innovativeness. The above-mentioned features are characteristic of the informally operating opportunity-driven self-employed.

Conversely, the exclusion-driven informal self-employed are vulnerable in terms of a lack of self-confidence and low levels of subjective well-being. These individuals lack personal initiative, motivation and determination, creativeness and innovativeness, resolution, and persistence. They tend to feel less happy and less satisfied with life. They do not treat independence as a value because they are accustomed to being controlled by others (external locus of control); they find it difficult to make decisions, choices, and control their lives; in addition, they do not try to instill the values of independence and self-reliance in their children (Temkin, 2009). Another interesting psychological aspect is that these individuals often have a negative perception of their health (Temkin, 2009).

Tax morale. Williams and Horodnic (2015b) researched the relationship between a person's tax morale and informal self-employment in the context of those driven by exclusion and exit rationales. Their research disclosed that the informal self-employed driven by exclusion rationales have individual norms, values, and beliefs that do not align with the codified state laws and suggest that this determines their greater engagement in the informal economy. However, no significant association was identified between those voluntarily choosing to engage in the informal economy and their tax morale.

In conclusion, the general profile of an economic agent operating in the informal labor market covers a set of economic, demographic, and personal (ego) characteristics that reflect an agent's socio-economic status, personality, and environment. Economic factors are the major determinants of an agent's participation in the informal labor market, although it is recognized that the decision to operate informally can also be affected by an agent's demographic characteristics (education, place of residence, gender, age, marital status, social status, and ethnicity) as well as personal and behavioral characteristics.

Based on the above review of the literature, the exclusion-driven self-employed operating in the informal labor market commonly belong to households with low income and low saving potential, do low-skilled or manual work, lack the capital, working premises, materials, and adequate markets for formal independent activities. From their operation in the informal economy, they expect some income for surviving and family upkeep. They are characterized by low education, reside in poorer regions and peripheral rural areas, are older and female, can be divorced or with large families, belong to a lower stratum of society and may belong to ethnic minorities. These individuals lack managerial abilities, skills, and previous experience, they are vulnerable in terms of a lack of self-confidence and low levels of subjective well-being and have low tax morale.

Meanwhile, the opportunity-driven self-employed operating in the informal labor market commonly belong to more affluent households, are involved in skilled and unskilled work, and can finance their activities with own or borrowed capital. From informal operation, they expect higher profits and non-material benefits. They are characterized by higher college/university education or manual training, reside in more affluent regions and urban areas, by statistics are younger male that can be separated, divorced or widowed, belong to a higher stratum of society, are local residents. They possess managerial and specific skills and abilities as well as sufficient previous experience, are self-confident with internal locus of control and unidentified tax morale. Nevertheless, since the results of previous studies concerning characteristics of those operating in the informal labor market are sometimes contradictory, a deeper analysis of the issue would be relevant.

2.3 The Causes of Informality

Before providing a detailed analysis of the causes of informality, it is relevant to note that in this book, there is a desire to identify how the causes of informality differ between regions. Here, a region is not treated as a group of countries sharing economic criteria (e.g., industrialization, urbanization or the level of development in individual industries), but as a state administrative unit established by the political decision of the central government, thus distributing the powers of self-government and dividing a country into small administrative territorial units. Given that the study is going to compare rural and urban regions (municipalities), it is relevant here to review not only the general causes of informality, but also to compare how the causes of informality differ in both types of administrative units - in rural and urban municipalities, characterized by different economic features.

According to Gadsby and Samson (2016), when attempting to distinguish between rural and urban informal economies, it is quite difficult to define what a rural area is and its distinctive features. Reimer and Bollman (2009a) refer to the rural population as the population of small towns and villages and note that separation of rural and urban territories is commonly related to the distance of an area from large cities and the population density. With reference to du Plessis et al. (2002), a rural area can also be referred to as a separate social unit with its own inherent population's mentality, history, way of life, and institutions. Summarizing different interpretations, it should be noted that in the framework of this study, a rural area is defined as an area characterized by a small population and a low population density, which is remote from urban areas and described by a specific identity as well as specific socio-cultural ties.

The concept of urban informality is not limited to informal economic activities in poor urban neighborhoods. It refers to the behavior, life, and work style of the entire urban population, access to services and realization of rights through informal channels (Banks et al., 2020). Roy (2005) defines urban informality as "a state of exception from the formal order of urbanization" (Roy, 2005, p. 147). In other words, urban informality refers to the activities and practices that fall outside state regulation. As noted by Ranganathan (2014), urban informality is flexible, and can occur through multiple channels, experiences, and strategies.

Previous studies widely acknowledge that there are multiple causes of informality which, according to Ulyssea (2020), can be static or dynamic by nature. Since both rural and urban economies are a part of the general economy, their informal sectors are affected by the general determinants of the informal economy. Nevertheless, it should not be overlooked that apart from the general determinants, informality in either urban or rural areas is also affected by their specific features as well as historical traditions. Given that the study focuses on the links between unemployment and the informal economy in rural and urban municipalities, we will provide the comparison of the general, rural, and urban-specific determinants of informality (see Table 2.3).

The summary in Table 2.3 shows that the major determinants of informality can be attributed to the categories of economic, regulation, market, public sector, social, and financial market determinants.

Economic determinants. At both the rural and urban levels, informality is primarily affected by the general economic factors, the significance of which is recognized by virtually all authors who have addressed the problems of the informal economy. In other words, the trends of informality are a consequence of the general state of the economy: if the general state of the economy is poor, informal activities can generate more advantages than disadvantages, and during periods of economic crises, economic agents are forced to look for more attractive niches for their activities (Elmurodov et al., 2020).

Ruge's (2010) research in 35 countries revealed that as much as 93% of the variation in the informal economy can be explained by a country's level of prosperity and economic development. High rates of GDP and per capita income, reflecting a high level of economic development, reduce the level of informality because economic agents are less inclined to operate in a riskier informal sector when they earn a stable and sufficiently high income, and vice versa.

Fiess et al. (2010) found the relationship between informal self-employment and macroeconomic fluctuations. In their flexible two-sector model, which was empirically adjusted to the cases of Argentina, Brazil, Colombia, and Mexico, the formal labor market was incorporated into the macro-model developed for a small economy. The research revealed that different types of economic shocks that cause macroeconomic fluctuations have a significant effect on the fluctuations in the variables in question, and these fluctuations are largely determined by the relative income

Table 2.3 Comparative analysis of the general, rural and urban-specific determinants of informality

General determinants of informality	Rural determinants of informality	Urban determinants of informality	Literature sources
Economic determinants			
A country's welfare level, a country's development level, a country's social security system development level, macroeconomic fluctuations, unemployment, relative income, relative sector size, real exchange rate, relative demand and productivity, government expenditure, debt-to-GDP ratio	Global, regional, and local economic climate, regional welfare, regional development level, regional social security system development level, availability of resources, demand size and structure, VAT tariffs for food stuff, exchange rates in neighboring countries, consumption, supply, trade indicators	Level of urbanization, globalization, general economic growth, GDP per capita, PPP, stage of economic development, unemployment rate, tertiarization of industries, income earning opportunities, historical number of agricultural workers, size of the rural informal sector	Alanon and Gomez-Antonio (2005), Perry et al. (2007), Gonenc and Tanrivermis (2007), Oviedo et al. (2009), Fialova (2010), Fiess et al. (2010), Ruge (2010), Gapšys and Eičaitė (2010), Chambwera et al. (2012), Kavan (2013), Pocius (2015), Weng (2015), Hassan (2016), Williams and Bezeredi (2017), Elmurodov et al. (2020), Huang et al. (2020)
Regulation determinants			
High tax tariffs, strict tax control, complexity of the taxation system, tax "gaps," complexity of the legal system, weak legal framework, strict labor regulations, complicated business formalization procedures, minimum wage requirement, regulation of social and health insurance systems and tax tariffs, regulation of benefits and allowances	(In)compatibility of regulatory provisions with the objectives of economic operators, governmental neglect of the resilience and dynamism typical of the informal economy to grant that informal activities serve as shock absorbers during the periods of market downturns	Provision and regulation of the support benefits and allowances (pensions), regulation of land use and building standards, citizens' ability to manage either formal or informal regulatory policies to retain a desired degree of autonomy	Biderman et al. (2008), Oviedo et al. (2009), Tokman (2011), Andrews et al. (2011), Chambwera et al. (2012), Vorley et al. (2012), Abdih and Medina (2013), Kavan (2013), Bosch and Campos-Vazquez (2014), Lesnik et al. (2014), Schneider et al. (2015), Nagac (2015), Kundt (2017), Banerjee et al. (2017), Medina and Schneider (2017) Gerard and Gonzaga (2018), Elmurodov et al. (2020), Ulyssea (2020), Banks et al. (2020)
Market determinants			

(continued)

Table 2.3 (continued)

General determinants of informality	Rural determinants of informality	Urban determinants of informality	Literature sources
Growing competition, increased market opportunities, limited resources, high market entry costs, consumer demand, minimal investment under risk conditions	Price factor, informal intermediation, informal trade rules, links with formal value chains, demand intensity	Cost pressure, unreasonably high land and real estate prices, continuous links between the formal and informal sectors, distorted value chains	Oviedo et al. (2009), OECD (2009), Minot (2011), Srija and Shirke (2014), Benson et al. (2014), Brown et al. (2014), Weng (2015), Smolka (2019), Banks et al. (2020)
Public sector determinants			
Distrust in public authorities, low institutional quality, public sector services and their quality, share of jobs in the public sector, bureaucracy level, corruption level, low probability of detection of informal activities, meager penalties for informal activities, low monitoring and enforcement, poor public administration, informal activity legalization processes	Regional infrastructure, optimization of public service provision (regionalization of rural areas), poor administration of natural resources, poor administration of land	Housing conditions, access to urban services, lack of sufficient social housing programs, inadequate public investment in urban infrastructure, informal service provision between a state and its citizens, poor urban planning, poor collective organization, large areas with informal housing and settlements	Perry et al. (2006), Oviedo et al. (2009), Reimer and Bollman (2009b), Tafenau et al. (2010), Schneider et al. (2010), Bihunirwa et al. (2012), Putzel et al. (2013), Benson et al. (2014), Brown et al. (2014), Enste (2015), Gadsby and Samson (2016), Williams and Bezeredi (2017), Smolka (2019), Sandoval et al. (2019), Mabakeng (2020), Banks et al. (2020)
Social determinants			
Public values, low level of public awareness, the distinction between personal and common (state) property	High economic (income) inequality, low level of human capital, public tax morale, social ties among community members	Soaring urban population, rural-urban income gap, percentage of urban slum population, low standard of living, non-payment of wages, social interactions	Reimer (2000), Barrett et al. (2001), Feld and Frey (2007), Oviedo et al. (2009), Torgler and Schneider (2009), Kavan (2013), Lithuanian Free Market Institute (2015), Sandoval et al. (2019), Smolka (2019), Banks et al. (2020), Elmurodov et al. (2020), Huang et al. (2020)
Financial market determinants			

(continued)

Table 2.3 (continued)

General determinants of informality	Rural determinants of informality	Urban determinants of informality	Literature sources
Unavailability of loans and credits, a country's financial market development level	Undeveloped credit markets, credit restrictions	Unavailability of affordable financing, poor financing infrastructure, restricted participation of private financial institutions	Blackburn et al. (2012), Kavan (2013), Tang and Guo (2017)

Source: compiled by the authors

earned by the salaried or self-employed, the relative size of the sector where the salaried or self-employed operate, and the real exchange rate.

High unemployment rates lead to intensification of informal activities because the unemployed are more likely to engage in informality when looking for alternatives to unemployment benefits or any other sources of income. This situation is the opposite of the situation when unemployment rates are low, and the chances of finding a formal job are high. Close links between the informal economy and informal employment are confirmed by for example Perry et al. (2007), Fialova (2010), and Pocius (2015). According to Fialova (2010), when the unemployment rate is high, economic agents can find it difficult to get involved into the formal labor market due to both a lack of opportunities and perceived monetary or non-monetary benefits. It should be noted that the impact of operating in the informal labor market on the size of the informal economy is much less significant in developed than in developing economies due to a wider potential of formal employment (Oviedo et al., 2009). Previous studies also indicate the dependence of informal self-employment on a stage of an economic cycle, which means that informal self-employment is affected by the relative demand and productivity shocks (Fiess et al., 2010). Oviedo et al. (2009) additionally single out poor access to resources (e.g., land, raw materials, financial resources).

In rural areas, the local, regional, and global economic climate is treated as a significant economic determinant of informality because it affects sales of rural production (in particular, agricultural products) in local, national, and international markets (for instance, soaring grain prices in international markets compared with grain prices in the local market can make the informal trade in foreign markets attractive, at least partly, to local grain growers). Previous studies also show that informal agricultural activities are undertaken as an alternative source of income during periods of economic downturn in a country or region (Chambwera et al., 2012). Weng (2015) highlights the impact of the local demand: according to the author, low-income consumers generate the demand for cheaper food and timber than in the formal market, and thus promote informal activities of regional farmers, foresters, and local communities. By selling their products cheaply, small rural companies or individual farmers do not expect to make the profit sufficient to cover the costs of activity transfer and operating in the formal sector; thus, the conduct of an informal activity becomes a logical solution. According to Gapšys and Eičaitė

(2010), informal agricultural activities in rural areas are affected by VAT tariffs on foodstuff and exchange rates in neighboring countries. While assessing the threat of the informal economy in various agricultural subsectors, the authors highlight the significance of consumption, supply, price level, and trade indicators. Gonenc and Tanrivermis (2007) revealed that the size of the informal economy in Turkish rural areas is affected by such factors as the usage of unpaid labor force, own consumption, and informal sales.

Informality in urban areas is statistically significantly affected by the general economic growth, the historic size of the number of agricultural workers, the size of the rural informal sector, and the urban–rural income gap (Kavan, 2013). Huang et al.'s (2020) research of the urban informal economies in China mainly associates urban informality with globalization of urban economies, the stages of a country's economic development, unemployment rate, and tertiarization of industries. Thus, the results of previous studies confirm the interrelationship between urban and rural informality.

Regulation determinants. Based on Loayza et al.'s (2006) study, the complexity of formal business regulation can be one of the main causes of informality. When researching the general causes of informality in the category of regulatory determinants, Schneider et al. (2010), Andrews et al. (2011), Abdih and Medina (2013), Lesnik et al. (2014), Schneider et al. (2015), Kundt (2017), and Medina and Schneider (2017) note the negative impact of a poorly formed tax system framework. The major features of a poorly formed tax system are vagueness of tax laws, "gaps" in tax laws, many tax types, and high tax rates. The method of simple regression, employed by Schneider et al. (2010), disclosed the negative relationship between tax tariffs and GDP. These results were later confirmed by Schneider et al. (2015), and Medina and Schneider (2017). Other studies, however, reveal no relationship between tax rates and the prevalence for the informal economy (Williams & Horodnic, 2016).

In addition to factors related to the taxation system, regulation determinants also cover unreasonably strict labor regulations and complicated business formalization procedures. The impact of these determinants on the size of the informal economy was confirmed by Oviedo et al. (2009), Feld and Schneider (2010), Tokman (2011), Nagac (2015), and the Lithuanian Free Market Institute (2015). Ulyssea (2020) notes that under extremely strict labor market regulation, informal employment not only helps to evade taxes, but also offers the benefits of flexible working hours.

Moreover, the requirement for a minimum wage can also be a factor promoting informal employment. In formal workplaces, the minimum wage represents a substantial share of the labor costs, so employers may not be willing to create new establishments if they lack the working capital to cover labor costs. In the latter case, the period during which an unemployed person can find a job is lengthened, which makes informal work an attractive alternative (Ulyssea, 2020). Bosch and Campos-Vazquez (2014) reveal that the start of a social security system in Mexico in 2002 led to an increase in informal employment because the system granted universal health insurance for all workers, including informal operators previously not entitled to health insurance, thus pushing down the costs of informality. Gerard and

Gonzaga (2018) found that generous unemployment insurance and benefit systems have a similar effect, and Banerjee et al. (2017) disclosed that this is also the case in countries that apply governmental benefit (cash) schemes which, while generating social benefits through public education, poverty reduction and better access to health care, can act as a factor that diminishes motivation of the members of society to work. Others, however, reveal that greater social protection measures reduce the prevalence of the informal economy (Bonnet et al., 2019a, 2019b; ILO, 2002; Williams & Horodnic, 2015a, 2015b).

In the rural context of informality, the factor of the population's response to regulatory interventions means that economic agents operating in rural areas assess the extent to which the regulation of their activity area meets personal needs and interests rather than state-level interests. For instance, if business registration is not complicated, business and tax laws are understandable and so forth, economic agents tend to comply with regulatory requirements. Otherwise, they tend to adjust to new informal business rules (Weng, 2015). In addition, Chambwera et al. (2012) and Vorley et al. (2012) note that informal activities in rural areas can be promoted by the government's disregard of the resilience and dynamism inherent in the informal economy. If the government tolerates informal activities and does not undertake any measures to reduce the size of the informal economy, but expect the informal sector to act as a shock absorber during the periods of the market downturn (in particular, with regard to most vulnerable population groups), then this policy will lead to high unemployment rates, more pronounced in rural than urban areas because a larger proportion of the socially vulnerable population tend to reside in rural areas.

In the urban context of informality, Kavan's (2013) study showed that a reduction of restrictions on the urban informal sector may help to enhance the capacity of this sector to absorb the growing labor force in the short and medium run. Nevertheless, it is also noted that this may run into opposition from the formal sector.

Biderman et al. (2008) provide evidence from Brazil that demonstrate the relationship between informality and regulation of land use and building standards. Agarwala (2013) argues that social wages (pensions) paid by Indian government to compensate construction workers for labor market informalization lead to the opposite results and end up in the growth of the informal labor market. Banks et al. (2020) note that urban citizens can manage either formal or informal regulatory policies and retain a degree of autonomy which is needed for informal operating.

Market determinants. The informal sector of the economy is relatively competitive because it is characterized by low barriers to market entry as well as relatively low operating costs, which allows informal operators to put competitive pressure on formally acting operators and even reduce the market power of formally acting companies. (OECD, 2009). According to Srija and Shirke (2014), informality is caused by growing competition, increased market opportunities, and limited resources. When competition is growing fiercer, reduction of operating costs is one of the most common methods to stay afloat because an economic agent can only expect profit growth by raising sales which are highly dependent on demand trends and the agent's ability to offer marketable products. In the first case, an economic agent may have little impact on the demand trends, while application of the second method may require time. Reduction of operating costs is an aspect that can be managed by an economic agent independently and sufficiently quickly. Thus, partial or complete informality is employed as a method to reduce operating costs. Similarly, high costs of entering the formal market can be attributed to the category of market determinants that promote informality (Oviedo et al., 2009).

Wider market opportunities can be associated with the potential to sell products and services either in the informal or in the formal sectors of the economy. Based on the OECD's (2009) study, informal economic agents can serve as suppliers of inputs to the formal sector. In addition, the products and services provided by informal operators raise the variety of products and services sold in the market. On the demand side, consumers tend to buy products even when they know or suspect that they are buying them from an informal operator. This is especially true when discussing agricultural products, because in this case, consumers tend to buy products at a lower price or want to be sure that they are buying an organic product rather than care about the degree of legitimacy of a supplier's activities. This approach, in its turn, significantly reduces a supplier's risk. The risk of operating in the informal market is also diminished by the fact that the investment required to start-up/conduct an informal activity does not appear to be high, and the risk of being caught and penalized is low (i.e., the cost of failure is lower than the cost of investment).

In the rural context of informality, market determinants are closely linked to the price determinant: when low global prices of agricultural products reduce rural farmers' earnings, they are forced to look for alternative sources of income (Minot, 2011), and thus may find informal activities attractive, providing higher profit margins that those in the formal economy. Informal activities not only help rural operators make more money (because informal traders offer better product purchase prices), but also allow barriers to be overcome such as high debt repayment rates and a lack of information on product purchase prices (Minot, 2011). In addition, informal traders offer timely cash settlements, there are lower transportation costs, less stringent quality control, and there is much room for flexibility (Vorley et al., 2015).

A growing number of low-income consumers, who demand low-cost products, promote informal agricultural activities in rural areas (Benson et al., 2014). In the category of market determinants, informality can also be promoted by the factors that are related to the functioning of product sales channels - intermediation of informal entities, informal trade rules, relations with formal value chains and/or demand intensity (Weng, 2015).

When analyzing the issues of urban informality, Banks et al. (2020) found that the pressure to reduce wage costs in competitive markets caused the informal labor markets to rise in the global north. Smolka (2019) emphasizes the impact of extremely high land and real estate prices typical of cities. According to the author, the poverty factor alone does not fully explain the existence of informality. Free market prices reflect the level at which a buyer can and is willing to pay for a particular good or service, and that level must be commensurate with the ability of a supplier to sell a good or service. If the two above-mentioned factors are not synchronized, some activities can be expected to be carried out informally. Extremely high land and real estate prices make these resources difficult to access for formal operators, which leads to informal land and real estate leasing markets, and some urbanized land being kept vacant intentionally, thus reducing the supply of these resources and keeping their formal prices high.

Brown et al. (2014) note that the rapid growth of urban informality in the context of the ongoing global (formal) economic crises is largely due to the continuous relationship between the formal and informal sector production, distribution and employment (i.e., a part of the production, distribution and employment are carried out formally and some informally on a subcontracting basis). Since this relationship is continuous, it distorts value chains over time, thus making the conduct of formal activities alone impossible in principle.

Public sector determinants. Williams and Bezeredi's (2017) research disclosed that the group of the exclusion-driven informal self-employed is characterized by a statistically significant correlation between the exit rationales of these economic agents and the vertical and horizontal trust in public authorities. Distrust in public authorities can be caused by corruption, weak rule of law and a lack of accountability, and low quality of public services in terms of infrastructure, social protection, and so forth (Oviedo et al., 2009). These are so-called governance factors.

According to Tafenau et al. (2010) and Schneider et al. (2010), the impact of public infrastructure determinants on informality can be bidirectional: a well-developed public infrastructure can offer better quality public services and thus motivate economic agents to operate transparently; on the other hand, an unreasonably large public sector performs its functions with difficulties. In the latter case, a bureaucracy and corruption-favorable environment is created, which, in its turn, reduces the quality of public services and pushes entrepreneurs into the informal sector. According to Enste (2015), the quantity and quality of public inspections can also have a significant impact on the size of the informal economy. If inspections are unreasonably frequent and the work quality of public officials is poor, entrepreneurs begin to avoid inspections by escaping to the informal sector.

The other determinants of informality that are also related to poor functioning of the public sector are a low probability of detection and a low fear of being punished for the conduct of informal economic activities. The significance of the above-mentioned determinants was confirmed in Williams and Bezeredi's (2017) study which revealed that the informal self-employed are not commonly characterized by a fear that their informal activities will be detected, nor are they characterized by a fear of punishment for the conduct of informal activities. In other words, there is no significant association between the level of penalties and probability of detection and the likelihood of participation in the informal economy.

In the rural context of informality, Perry et al. (2006) and Putzel et al. (2013) found that distrust in public authorities is greatest in those areas where the residents suffer from income inequalities and the limited access to resources (e.g., when public authorities support only large businesses, monopolies, and oligopolies). The distrust is even increasing when the access to particular resources (mainly land and water bodies) is granted only to a limited elite circle (Benson et al., 2014) and/or when resource management is poor (Mabakeng, 2020).

The above-described policies create preconditions for unfair competition, which impedes operating in formal markets. Unfair competition, in its turn, leads to distrust of small rural entrepreneurs in public administration and lays the foundations for the development of informal culture. The style of governance has the same effect in the cases where public officials are aware of the operators that conduct informal activities, but tolerate these activities, often on the basis of corruption. According to Weng (2015), even those who have previously conducted formal activities may decide to escape to the informal sector due to the low quality of services provided by public authorities, the high level of bureaucracy, the excessive level of control or accountability, and so forth. Feeling powerless against the system, having no power to make rational operational decisions, and being dependent on factors beyond their control, small economic operators may begin to prioritize informal activities to supply the products to the market on their own conditions (Bihunirwa et al., 2012).

Informality in rural areas is significantly affected by the determinants of public infrastructure. Based on Gadsby and Samson's (2016) study, rural areas are characterized by the limited access to public infrastructure. For example, due to a long geographical distance or terrain conditions, there may be problems in installing and/or ensuring a mobile phone connection, internet connection, road transport communication, and so forth.

Optimization of public service provision (e.g., closing medical centers, branches of financial institutions, counseling centers in villages) leads to the decline in prosperity in rural areas. Although being focused on larger communities served, optimization of the public service provision seems at first sight to be a rational solution in terms of a public policy, it cannot be considered rational in terms of rural prosperity because it is raising the costs of public services (mainly, transport costs) to rural residents. In addition, with the loss of some public services, rural areas lose some of their autonomy. For example, branches of financial institutions operating in rural areas may be allowed to charge different (usually lower) fees, deposit and credit interest rates than those charged in urban areas. This causes difficulties concerning the identity of rural communities and raises dissatisfaction with governmental policies (Reimer & Bollman, 2009b), thus leading to higher rates of informal activities.

When researching the impact of the public sector determinants on urban informality, Smolka (2019) emphasizes the problems of the lack of sufficient social housing programs and inadequate public investment in urban infrastructure (for provision of public amenities and services (e.g., drainage and sewage systems). Banks et al. (2020) note that in four sub-Saharan African cities under consideration, the poor urban infrastructure leads to public and private water suppliers increasing their revenues by supplying water informally (spatial expansion of urban informality). The authors also note the negative effects of the so-called co-production. "Co-production" is referred to as a process of informal provision of services between a state and its citizens, which is formed when the planning process executed by the national government alone is not adequate. These findings are in line with Brown et al.'s (2014) study which discloses the links between informality and poor urban planning as well as poor collective organization. Brown et al. (2014) link the latter factors to the establishment of particular informal alliances and particular political spaces in which local governments neglect citizens' rights.

Sandoval et al. (2019) argue that informal housing and settlements are significant determinants of urban informality. Informal settlements are cut off from urban infrastructure and basic services, they can be an object of real estate speculation, and their residents are not protected by the state. As a result, the countries with large informal housing and settlement areas in their cities are often characterized by high levels of informal economic activities.

Social determinants. The impact of social determinants on informality manifests itself through social values, the level of awareness, the relationship between personal and common-use (state) property, and the relative interpretation of cultural, social, and legal norms. In a society with a low level of population's awareness about the costs of informality and benefits of formality, informal activities are much more likely to be considered acceptable than in a society with a high level of population awareness (Lithuanian Free Market Institute, 2015).

One of the most significant social causes of informality is low public tax morale (i.e., a high acceptability of tax evasion). Torgler and Schneider (2009) found that the World Values Survey's question on how justifiable people think it is to avoid paying taxes, which the researchers use as a measure of public tax morale, is highly correlated with other factors of the institutional environment (e.g., corruption, rule of law). According to Oviedo et al. (2009), public tax morale reflects the ability of the public sector to serve public interests when economic agents want to actively participate in a state's socio-economic system instead of belonging to marginal groups. As early as 1972, Allingham and Sandmo (1972) found that a population's tax compliance largely depends on them weighing up the costs and benefits of non-compliance and compliance. The benefits of tax evasion are determined by the individual's marginal tax level and real individual income. The expected costs of tax evasion depend on the deterrent measures imposed by the government (Feld & Frey, 2007). The low level of public awareness creates a dividing line between personal and common (state) property from a society's point of view: personal property and income are completely separated from a state's property and income, thus the obligation to pay taxes is treated not as a civic duty but as a deprivation of a part of personal income.

In the rural context, informality is significantly affected by high economic (income) inequality, low levels of human capital, and the social relationship in communities. According to the United States Department of Agriculture Economic Research Service (2021), in 2018 over 16% of people living in rural areas had an income below the federal poverty line, while those living in urban areas had a poverty rate of only 12.6%. Fears of poverty (or attempts to escape poverty) as well as the desire to diversify income often lead the rural areas to informality because informal activities are seen as a potential to escape poverty and diversify income (Barrett et al., 2001). In this manner, informal activities become a source of livelihood for families with financial difficulties.

Badita et al. (2015) note that despite many policies undertaken to promote the development of human capital in rural areas, the major issues that still have to be dealt with include insufficient investment in education and training as well as exclusion and workforce migration, which, in their turn, lead to stagnation or even deterioration of the human capital. The populations of small settlements and villages belonging to rural areas are often linked by similar sociodemographic features: kinship, living conditions, lifestyle, employment status, etc. All this serves to help the formation of close community ties: community members share resources, information, experiences, and can even feel communal responsibilities to each other (Reimer, 2000). Such social connections are not typical of urban communities. Close social ties among community members promote informal exchanges based on mutual trust, which, in its turn, fosters informality (Weng, 2015).

Regarding urban informality, Kavan (2013) argues that the growth of the urban informal sector is determined by the growing urban population; thus, it is difficult to reduce the size of the urban informal sector without dampening urban population growth. Huang et al. (2020) link urban informality to rural-urban income gap and rural-to-urban migration; the latter factor leads to the growth of the urban population, and thus confirms the relationship between the urban population growth and urban informality. Smolka (2019) denies the relationship between rural-to-urban migration and urban informality and argues that even though the number of rural-to-urban migrants is decreasing, an urban informality rate remains relatively stable, which proposes that the two factors are not interrelated. Sandoval et al. (2019) provide the argument that a lower urban informality rate is a result of the lower percentage of urban slum population because this population group is exposed to social and economic hazards and have limited income opportunities, which pushes them into informality. Elmurodov et al. (2020) link urban informality to low standards of living which promote the conduct of hidden activities, high unemployment rates, and non-payment of wages that force a substantial share of the population to earn income in any other way, and thus facilitate informality.

Banks et al. (2020) highlight the importance of social relationship and social interactions. According to them, a substantial share of urban informality can be determined by social negotiations, conflicts, and practice. In the context of social interactions, the authors talk not only about the interaction of economic agents or stigmatization, but also about the interaction between a state and society through public service provision, regulation of labor markets, and urban governance.

Financial market determinants. The impact of financial market determinants on informality is primarily manifested through the availability of financing (loans, credits). It is closely related to the level of a country's financial system development and the intermediary functions of financial institutions. As noted by Blackburn et al. (2012), economic agents with heterogeneous skills seek external financing so that they can participate in investment projects. The asymmetry of information between lenders and borrowers in financial markets is inherent in financing contracts. When establishing these contracts, economic agents decide how much of their income (assets) they can offer as collateral, and how much of their income (assets) they will not declare to reduce their tax obligations. Thus, the marginal net benefit of income declaration reduces the likelihood of informality.

In the rural context, a crucial role is played by the availability of credits because credits not only finance the start-up or restructuring of a formal activity, but also facilitate economic transactions. If the potential of credit in a rural area is limited, economic operators may lack their own funds to start and run a formal activity. Underdeveloped credit markets and credit constraints not only increase the degree of informality but can also lead to the development of the informal rural credit market. Nevertheless, Tang and Guo's (2017) research revealed that even the financial flows generated by the informal rural credit market are not sufficient to meet the credit needs of rural areas. Kavan's (2013) study disclosed that lending to the rural sector has a positive impact not only on the rural sector itself, but also on the urban sector because the policies of granting credits to the rural sector have some dampening impact on the urban informality growth.

The lack of funding is not limited to rural areas. The report provided by International International Institute for Environment and Development (2019) reveals that most urban residents do not have any access to affordable long-term financing. Developing countries have poor financing infrastructures, the expansion of which is often hampered by the political decisions to restrict participation of the private sector (financial institutions, savings and credit cooperatives, estate developers, etc.). It should be noted that involvement of the private sector could help to mobilize complementary resources, share risks, and foster fiscal and non-fiscal incentives.

In conclusion, at both the rural and urban levels, informality is strongly affected by **general economic determinants,** the significance of which is recognized by virtually all authors who have researched the informal economy. In other words, informal tendencies are a consequence of the general state of the economy: if the general economic state is poor, informal activities can generate more advantages than disadvantages. During crisis periods, economic agents are forced to look for more attractive niches for their activities, and the informal sector can appear to be an attractive niche. The complexity of formal **business regulation** can be one of the main causes of informal employment. In the rural context of informality, the factor of the population's response to regulatory interventions means that economic agents operating in rural areas assess the extent to which the regulation of their activity area meets personal needs and interests rather than state-level interests. In the urban context, the relationship between informality and regulation of land use and building standards can be observed. From **a market perspective**, informality is determined by cost reduction and fierce market competition pressures. In the rural context, low prices of agricultural products reduce farmers' wages, so they are forced to look for alternative (informal) sources of income. With regard to urban informality, it can be rising due to the pressure to reduce wage costs and the extremely high land and real estate prices inherent in cities. The major **public sector determinants** of informality are corruption, weak rule of law and a lack of accountability, and low quality of public services (in terms of infrastructure, social protection, etc.). In the rural context, distrust in public authorities is greatest in the areas where the residents suffer from income inequality and the limited access to resources. In addition, rural areas tend to have the limited access to public infrastructure. In the urban context, informality can be additionally determined by the problems of the lack of sufficient social housing programs and inadequate public investment in urban infrastructure. The impact of **social determinants** on informality manifests itself through social values, the level of awareness of the costs of informality and benefits of formality, the relationship between personal and common (state) property, and the relative interpretation of cultural, social, and legal norms. In the rural context, informality is significantly affected by high economic (income) inequality, low levels of human capital, and close social ties in communities. The growth of the urban informal sector is determined by soaring urban population, the rural–urban income gap, rural-to-urban migration, and a high percentage of urban population in informal settlements. The impact of **the financial market determinants** on informality is primarily manifested through the availability of financing (loans, credits). It is closely related to the level of a country's financial system development and the intermediary functions of financial institutions. In the rural context, a crucial role is played by the availability of credit because credit not only finances the start-up or restructuring of a formal activity, but also facilitate economic transactions. Urban informality can be determined by the poor financing infrastructure and the political decisions restricting participation of the private sector (financial institutions, savings and credit cooperatives, estate developers, etc.).

2.4 Classification of the Most Common Forms of Informal Employment

As mentioned earlier, the informal economy can be conceptualized as "the total number of informal jobs, whether carried out in formal sector enterprises, informal sector enterprises, or households, during a given reference period" (the definition provided by the 17th ICLS, cited by Hussmanns (2004), p. 5). This view captures the heterogeneity of contexts within which informal employment can occur. By informal employment if meant paid work that is "*de facto* or *de jure* not subject to national labor legislation, income taxation or entitlement to social protection or certain other employment benefits (advance notice of dismissal, severance pay, paid annual or sick leave, etc.)" (OECD Development Centre, 2019, p. 26). Table 2.4 provides a classification of the most common forms of informal employment based on several characteristics.

When the different forms of informality are classified by ***the subject*** involved in an economic activity, informally operating economic agents can be categorized as informally operating economic units (i.e., *legal entities*) and workers (i.e., *natural persons*). Informal economic units – enterprises – are defined as non-incorporated private enterprises producing at least partially for the market but without a formal bookkeeping system or not registered to national relevant authorities (Bonnet et al., 2019a). Informally operating natural persons can act as informal employees (informally hired persons), own-account workers (in the latter case, they, like informal

Table 2.4 Classification of the most common forms of informal employment by a typical characteristic

Characteristic	Forms of informal employment	Author(s), year
By a subject	Informal economic units, workers in the informal economy	Hussmanns (2004); Avirgan et al. (2005), ILO (2015), Abraham (2017), Bonnet et al. (2019a)
By employment status	Employees, employers, own-account workers (including unpaid family workers and workers producing goods for own final use)	Hussmanns (2004), Temkin (2009), Karabchuk and Nikitina (2011), Zimmermann (2012), ILO (2015), Lehmann and Pignatti (2018), Bonnet et al. (2019a)
By (in)voluntary nature of operation in the formal or informal labor market	Voluntary operating in the informal labor market sector, involuntarily operating in the informal labor market sector	Dohmen et al. (2010), Lehmann and Pignatti (2018)
By the degree of (non)formalization	Registered, unregistered, partly registered	OECD (2002), OECD (2008), Temkin (2009), Schneider (2012), OECD Development Centre (2019)
By the form of settlement (payment)	Barter of goods and services, mutual self-help, odd jobs, direct sale/service activities, unpaid relatives, cash, bank transfers with a falsified purpose of payment	Williams (1996), Temkin (2009), Dohmen et al. (2010), Weng (2015)
By activity premises (activity space)	Identifiable, unidentifiable	OECD (2002), Renshaw (2002), Hussmanns (2004), Bureau and Fendt (2011), Weng (2015), Chen and Sinha (2016), Shapland and Heyes (2017), Martinez et al. (2017), Truong (2018), OECD Development Centre (2019), Bhan et al. (2020), WIEGO (2020)

Source: compiled by the authors

enterprises, carry out officially unregistered income-generating economic activities) and contributing family workers (these natural persons are not initiators of informal economic activities; they perform the functions of assistants, but are also classified as persons having an informal job) (OECD, 2019). What unites the above-mentioned legal and natural entities and persons is that, from both a legal and a practical point of view, their activities are not covered or are insufficiently covered by formal arrangements.

When the different forms of informality are classified by ***employment status***, economic agents operating in the informal labor market are categorized as employees, employers, and own-account workers. Informal *employees* are defined as economic agents that have informal jobs and their employment relationship is not subject to national labor legislation. The income earned by informal employees is not reported, and thus is not subject to income or social security taxation. Informal employees are not socially protected. For example, they are not entitled to the relevant benefits in the event of incapacity for work due to sickness, maternity/paternity, old age, disability or in other cases provided for by national social security laws; they are not entitled to the benefits from annual paid leave and paid sick leave. By considering the above-mentioned features, ILO (2015) distinguishes the following groups of informal employees:

- workers without explicit written employment contracts that are not subject to labor legislation;
- workers who do not benefit from paid annual or sick leave or social security and pension schemes because their income is not reported;
- paid domestic workers employed by households without labor or service provision contracts;
- casual, short-term, and seasonal workers.

With reference to the definition, provided by the 17th ICLS, informal *employers* have informal jobs in their own enterprises operating in the informal sector of the economy or hire informal employees (self-employed with employees) - permanent or casual, short- or long-term, seasonal workers, low-paid, lacking social protection, health benefits, legal status, rights and freedom of association (ILO, 2003; Zimmermann, 2012). According to Hussmanns (2004), "an enterprise" in this context refers to any unit that is engaged in production of goods or provision of services for sale or barter. Following the ILO's (2015) categorization, members of informal producers' cooperatives (not established as legal entities) may also be attributed to the group of employers. Based on the RLMS data, Karabchuk and Nikitina (2011) define informal employers as those who work in firms with less than five employees, who report not working in a firm/organization, and who report not having any official labor contracts.

Own-account workers may also work in their own informal sector enterprises, but with no employees, or operate as freelance service providers. Based on the statistical data provided by Bonnet et al. (2019a), own-account workers constitute a large proportion of the informal workforce. In 2016, in the group of developed countries, it accounted for 67.2% of total informal employment excluding the agricultural sector, and 68.8% of total informal employment including the agricultural sector (see Fig. 2.1). Over two-thirds of the informal workforce, therefore, are own-account workers. Meanwhile, the share of employers accounted for almost a third of total informal employment, and the share of waged employees for nearly 10% of total informal employment.

The own-account informal worker category also covers unpaid (or contributing) family workers whose jobs are informal by nature regardless of whether an enterprise or an employer for which they work operates formally or informally (ILO, 2015; Bonnet et al., 2019a). In addition, the group of own-account workers incorporates those who produce particular goods exclusively for their own final use or the use by their household (ILO, 2015). According to Temkin (2009), the rationale behind this categorization is that the informal self-employed, or own-account workers, are incipient entrepreneurs.

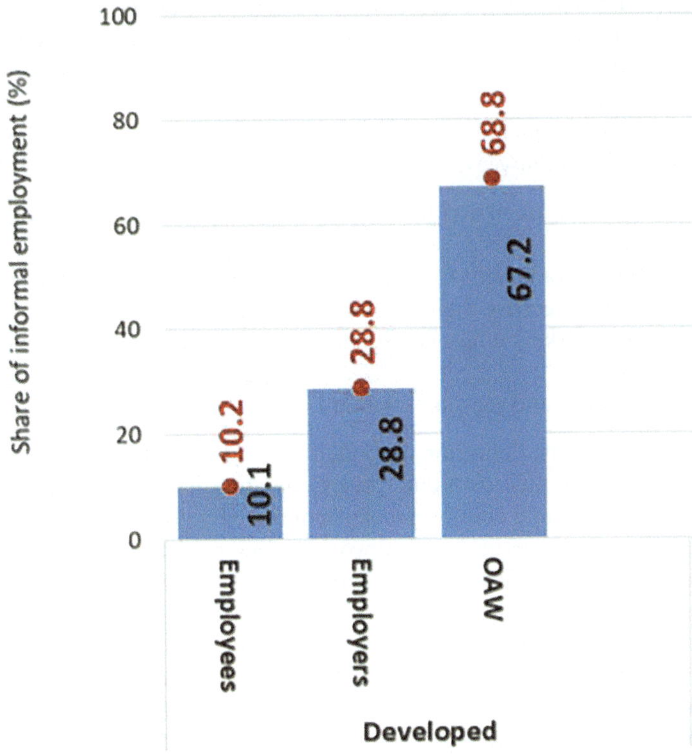

Fig. 2.1 Shares of persons attributable to different employment status groups in total informal employment including the agricultural sector in developed countries in 2016, %
Source: Bonnet et al., 2019a, p. 12

When the different forms of informality are classified by ***the (in)voluntary nature of operation*** in the formal or informal labor market segment, informal activities can be categorized as either voluntary or involuntary. Dohmen et al. (2010) note that the decision to engage in informal employment either voluntarily or involuntarily is usually made or can be made by employer-dependent workers. According to Lehmann and Pignatti (2018), when workers are pushed out of the formal labor market into the informal one against their will, then the labor market is considered segmented, and workers' quality of life, and thus their well-being, deteriorate. When persons are free to choose whether to operate in the formal or informal labor market, then the labor market is integrated, and while there is always a certain percentage of informal employment, workers' quality of life, and well-being are increasing. This classification of informal workers as either exclusion- or exit-driven into the informal economy, as already discussed, is discussed in a vast literature on the informal economy.

When the different forms of informality are classified by ***the degree of (non) formalization,*** informal jobs or activities can be categorized as registered, unregistered (OECD, 2002), or partly registered. For instance, the category of registered work covers economic agents that have formal employment contracts but work informally after formal working hours, at weekends, on holidays, work a part of their official working hours informally (so-called non-billing work).

Completely informal activities can be conducted by one person, a group of related persons or the same household (family). With reference to the estimations provided by the OECD Development Centre (2019), the percentages of different economic agents in the total number of informally operating persons are as follows: 45% of informal workers are the informal self-employed, 36% are employees, 16% - contributing family workers, and less than 3% are employers.

Temkin (2009) argues that although informal activities can be conducted by both economic operators with formal employment contracts and the ones without formal employment contracts, the latter are more vulnerable because they are not entitled to any social security; they are attributable to the highest level of informality, and this operation mode only further strengthens the informal nature of employment. Economic operators attributable to less socially vulnerable groups and intermediate levels of formality are not characterized by all, but 1–2 features of informality.

Previous studies suggest that the level of informality is particularly high among own-account workers and the self-employed (OECD, 2008). For instance, Lehmann and Terrell (2005) found that more than half own-account workers in the Czech Republic make no social contributions at all, while Breach et al.'s (2006) research revealed that income tax evasion rate among informally operating entrepreneurs and professionals is as high as 77%.

When the different forms of informality are classified by ***the form of settlement (payment),*** the major forms of informal employment are as follows: barter of goods and services, mutual self-help, odd jobs, and direct sale/service activities (Dohmen et al., 2010) which are mostly settled in cash. When conducting informal economic activities, bank transfers are less frequent since the income generated by these activities is sought to be concealed from authorities. Even when making bank transfers, the actual purpose of a payment is falsified (e.g., by indicating "replenishment of the account," "repayment of debt").

Williams (1996) found that the unemployed can participate in the informal labor market through the so-called local exchange trading systems (LETS), especially at the community level. The basis for the operation of these systems is informal exchange. The system itself works as follows: informal economic agents belonging to the system (groups, communities, associations, etc.) exchange goods and services without using money as a means of payment. Temkin (2009) notes that family members and relatives assisting an informal economic agent are not paid at all, although they are also considered participants of the informal labor market.

According to Weng (2015), in the case of informal employment in the agricultural sector, the main means of payment are cash, and sometimes barter. They allow participants of the informal economy to hide their tax revenues. Farm workers and small entrepreneurs do not declare their income or declare only a part of it, and no registers related to official employment of farm workers are kept.

Finally, in the context of the forms of informal employment ***by activity premises (activity space)***, it must be noted that informal activities can be conducted either inside or outside an economic agent's home, activity premises can be identifiable, unidentifiable or an activity may have no fixed location (Hussmanns, 2004). Economic operators working at home (or near the home) typically might sew or repair clothing, footwear, engage in traditional crafts, food production, laundry, assemble and repair electrical and electronic appliances, automobiles, provide beauty, childcare, education, and other services (OECD, 2002; Bureau & Fendt, 2011; Chen & Sinha, 2016; Bhan et al., 2020). Bureau and Fendt (2011) argue that this sector is important due to its relatively significant financial weight and strong family cohesion. According to WIEGO (2020), a portion of these economic agents sell goods or services directly to markets, while others are sub-contracted and produce work on a piece-rate basis for domestic or global supply chains. Activities in this sector often go beyond closed communities and are carried out with participation of a few or tens of households, independently of the market economy (Renshaw, 2002).

Economic operators acting in public spaces primarily include street vendors (Martinez et al., 2017; Truong, 2018; CGAP, 2020; WIEGO, 2020, etc.). These operators trade a wide variety of foods and industrial goods. Other common forms of informal employment in public spaces are work in restaurants and hotels, subcontracted janitors and security guards, casual laborers in the construction sector, piece-rate workers in sweatshops, temporary office helpers or offsite data processors (WIEGO, 2020), workers in the financial sector, personal service sector, entertainment and catering sector (Shapland & Heyes, 2017). WIEGO's (2020) report also indicates that economic agents acting in public spaces include the workers in the transport sector (taxi drivers, cart pullers, bicycle peddlers, rickshaw pullers, etc.) as well as waste pickers (people who collect waste and earn some money by taking this waste to recycling centers).

Based on the OECD Development Centre's (2019) report, a significant part of informal employment is observed in the agricultural sector where economic agents are involved in cultivating fruit and vegetables, cereals, floriculture, fisheries, livestock, and poultry farming, etc. The above-mentioned agricultural products are usually sold within rural communities or close to the place of residence of informally operating economic agents (Weng, 2015). This is facilitated by close links among community members.

In conclusion, although the variety of the forms of informal employment is huge, this literature analysis has allowed a categorization of the most common forms of informal employment by subject, employment status, (in)voluntary nature of operation in the formal or informal labor market segment, the degree of (non)formalization, the form of settlement (payment), and activity premises (activity space). The close relationships observed among the above-mentioned categories as well as the ability of economic operators to easily change the activity forms and the activity sector reflect the integration of informal labor markets. The common features of virtually all forms of informality are a lack of legal recognition and work without security or social protection.

2.5 Informal Employment and Quality of Life

The topic of informal employment is commonly associated with developing economies and depicted as a sign of "backwardness." In recent decades, however, it has been recognized that informal employment is more widely prevalent and is an inherent part of contemporary capitalist economies rather than some leftover from pre-capitalist modes of production (Marcelli et al., 2010; Zimmermann, 2012; Williams & Horodnic, 2015b). One outcome has been that it has been recognized that the informal economy is not disappearing. The consequence has been that it has become more important to understand the broader impacts of informality. One such stream of research has been on the impacts of informality on the quality of life of participants in this realm.

It is widely recognized that informal employment can help economic agents increase their income and realize their potential, that it provides more freedom and flexibility, and enhances a sense of community, and that these benefits are common to both developing and developed economies (Marcelli et al., 2010). Consequently, informal employment might be deemed to serve not only the purely economic well-being of the economic agents involved in it, but also various other aspects of quality of life. When researching a population's quality of life, it is not common to focus upon the relationship between quality of life and informal employment. Nevertheless, given that informal employment is a part of the general labor market and that the prevalence of informal employment has tended to remain stable or is even growing in both developed and developing economies, it can be stated that informal employment has an impact on population's quality of life.

Quality of life is a broad concept that encompasses many different dimensions which, in their turn, reflect both objective factors of personal well-being, such as material resources, health, work status, living conditions, and many others, and a subjective understanding of various well-being factors, individual needs, and priorities. From an economic perspective, quality of life reflects a person's economic performance, material wealth, material needs, income, etc. (Chrenekova et al., 2016). However, economic indicators alone are not sufficient to measure social progress. Based on the Eurostat's (2020) framework, quality of life is measured by employing the following 9 (8+1) dimensions:

- Material living conditions;
- Productive or main activity;
- Health;

- Education;
- Leisure and social interactions;
- Economic security and physical safety;
- Governance and basic rights;
- Natural and living environment;
- Overall experience of life.

Material living conditions are represented by income, consumption, and material conditions. These indicators reflect economic agents' purchasing power, living conditions and provide the most complete perspective on the situation of households. *Productive or main activity* is represented by quantity of employment, quality of employment, and other main activities (inactive population and unpaid work). These indicators help to estimate the number of hours worked by economic agents, evaluate the balance between their working and non-working life, the safety and ethics situation. *Health* is represented by health outcome indicators (life expectancy, the number of healthy life years, subjective assessments of own health, chronical diseases, limitations in activity), health determinants (healthy and unhealthy behaviors), and access to health care. Health is considered one of the essential dimensions of the quality of life because poor health, either physical or mental (or both), has an extremely detrimental effect on subjective well-being. The dimension of *education* reflects the potential of citizens to make progress in the future because individuals with low education and low skills have fewer opportunities to find a job and, consequently, fewer prospects for economic prosperity. In the Eurostat's (2020) estimations, education is represented by population's educational attainment (including the number of early school leavers), self-assessed and assessed skills, participation in lifelong learning, and opportunities for education (rate of enrolment of pupils in pre-primary education).

The dimension of *leisure and social interactions* directly affects citizens' life satisfaction. It is represented by leisure activities (their quantity and quality) and social interactions, namely activities with other people – frequency of social contacts and satisfaction with personal relationships; contribution to others – volunteering in informal contexts; the potential to receive social support (help from others) and social cohesion (trust in others). The dimension of *economic security and physical safety* is represented by two sub-dimensions. First, economic security incorporates wealth (the value of assets owned minus the value of liabilities owed at a point in time by a household), and the ability to face unexpected expenses, having or not having arrears and the value of assets (especially of liquid type). Economic security is a crucial aspect of citizens' lives because it allows forward planning and helps overcome sudden economic and social shocks in the environment. Second, physical safety incorporates the number of homicides per country from police records and the proportion of those who perceive there is crime, violence or vandalism in the area. The dimension of *governance and basic rights* is represented by trust in institutions and public services, discrimination and equal opportunities, and active citizenship. This dimension contributes to quality of life by providing the right legislative guarantees for citizens, getting them involved in public debates, and thus shaping public policies.

The dimension of *natural and living environment* is represented by the objective and subjective indicators. The objective indicators include the amounts of pollutants present in the air and the values of particulate matter, while the subjective indicators cover individuals' own perceptions of noise levels, the existence of pollution and grime in their local area, their satisfaction with the environment and the green spaces in their local area. The factors of natural and living environment condition quality of life because they have a direct impact on both citizens' health and economic prosperity of a society. Finally, the dimension of a person's *overall experience of life* is represented by one's life satisfaction (cognitive appreciation), affect (a person's feelings or emotional states, both positive and negative) and eudemonics (a sense of having meaning and purpose in one's life, or good psychological functioning.).

The above-presented Eurostat's (2020) framework for evaluating quality of life indicates that unemployment or informal employment does not only mean a loss or increase in income, respectively, but also has other social and mental consequences that affect the quality of life of individuals and households.

The relationship between informal employment and quality of life can be viewed from two different perspectives. First, it can be treated as a lifetime earning potential. According to Zimmermann (2012), workers who start their working careers based on temporary or short-term work tend to work for lower pay, hence their lifetime earning potential is lower, and thus is lower standard of living and quality of life. In this way, both individuals and households earning income in the informal employment sector are at higher risk of poverty. In addition to lifetime earning potential, the other important elements of quality of life are material comfort, material well-being, and social security life (OECD, 2011). The latter are closely related to personal and/or household income and the type of this income (i.e., formal or informal income): better social protection is provided to persons earning formal wages because formal income serves as the basis for paying all taxes related to personal social security (sickness, unemployment, disability, maternity/paternity, widows/widowers, and orphan benefits, etc.). The results of some previous studies reflecting the impact of informal employment on the quality of life of economic agents are reviewed in Table 2.5.

Gonzalez-Baltazar et al.'s (2019) research of the situation in Mexico (the Metropolitan area of Guadalajara), based on a representative sample of 507 informal workers, showed that informal workers have relatively good economic benefits, evade taxes and have more flexibility with schedules. Nevertheless, they are characterized by a low level of satisfaction with the quality of working life, they report that operating informally, they lack occupational and health safety, many of them work in unhealthy conditions and are exposed to risks in the workplace. The survey included 48% of men and 52% of women; the predominant age group covered the respondents aged 15–29. As many as 67% of the respondents admitted working in the informal sector for 1–15 years. The findings concerning insufficiency of safety and health measures in informal employment are in line with Forastieri's (1999)

Table 2.5 Review of some previous findings concerning the effects of informal employment on economic agents' quality of life

Author(s), year	Research method	Country, period	Basic findings
Gonzalez-Baltazar et al. (2019)	Respondent survey	Mexico, 2019	Informal workers gain relatively good economic benefits, but there are problems with occupational safety and health
Dike (2019)	Labor force survey	Cambodia, 2012	Informal employment can significantly increase the risk of work injuries/diseases
Heitink et al. (2017)	Desk research, semi-structured interviews	The Netherlands, 2013–2014	Advantages – economic benefit, escape from home and satisfaction; disadvantages – burden of responsibility, physical and mental health problems
Chrenekova et al. (2016)	Nonparametric statistical tests, Kruskal-Wallis median test	Ukrainian regions, 2014	The ability of rural areas to create informal jobs does not raise population's material well-being and thus the quality of life
Alvarez et al. (2016)	WHOQOL-BREF questionnaire, frequency distributions and the chi-squared test	Colombia, 2012–2013	Elderly people's informal employment leads to higher quality of life in terms of physical and mental health and social connections
Kireenko and Nevzorova (2015)	Clustering, regression analysis	150 countries, 1999–2007	When informality level is increasing, the level of life is also increasing, but a long and healthy life and access to knowledge are decreasing
Rojas (2013)	Mid-size survey	Mexico, 2013	Informal employment is not associated with either better or worse quality of life compared to formal employment
Lehmann and Pignatti (2018)	Analysis of worker mobility, wage gap regressions, a panel across an interval, quantile regression	Ukraine, 2003-2004, 2003–2007	In segmented labor markets, quality of life is decreasing, while in integrated labor markets, quality of life can reach a much higher level
Pourreza et al. (2018)	Cross-sectional descriptive analysis, respondent survey	Iranian society, December 2016–July 2017	Quality of life of women working in the informal sector is significantly lower than that of women working in the formal sector
Bertranou et al. (2014)	Literature review, statistical data analysis, descriptive analysis	Argentina, 1990–2011	Job and life quality of the self-employed operating in the informal sector are promoted by deregulation, greater labor market flexibility and reduction in the cost of labor

(continued)

Table 2.5 (continued)

Author(s), year	Research method	Country, period	Basic findings
Cuevas et al. (2009)	Statistical data analysis, questionnaire survey	Indonesia, 2007	The mean monthly income of workers in the informal group is relatively lower than that of workers in the mixed group
Ruiz et al. (2017)	Health and quality of life survey	Chile, 2009–2010	There exists a consistent relationship between informal employment and poor self-rated health and mental health
Lopez-Ruiz et al. (2015)	Survey of working conditions and health, logistic regression models, adjusted odds ratios	Central America, 2011	About one-third of men and as many women report poor self-perceived health and poor mental health; it is associated with a lack of social security coverage
Pfau-Effinger (2017)	A unique survey data set from the National Statistical Office of Moldova	Moldova, 2008	The informal self-employed are low educated, often living on social benefits

Source: compiled by the authors

findings: they indicate that economic agents operating in the informal sector often do not have sufficient technical means and resources to comply with appropriate health and safety regulations. In addition, they often lack an understanding of the necessity for protection. This leads to a high risk of occupational accidents, diseases, and environmental hazards. The relationship between informal employment and occupational health was also analyzed by Dike (2019). By applying the 2012 Cambodia Labor Force Survey, the author found that informal employment is associated with a significant increase in the probability of work injury/illness.

Heitink et al.'s (2017) research in the Netherlands revealed that every sixth employee performs informal work tasks, and the number of persons working informally in the health care sector is even higher - every fourth employee. The major causes of informality are income, escape from home and satisfaction. In the context of quality of life, the respondents pointed to the burden of responsibility, the lack of independence and health (fatigue, physical and mental health) problems. The problems of low income and social isolation were also mentioned. The existence of a consistent relationship between informal employment and poor self-rated health and mental health was also confirmed by Ruiz et al. (2017), who carried out a health and quality of life survey in Chile over the 2009–2010 period, and Lopez-Ruiz et al. (2015), who analyzed the situation in Central America in 2011. The authors argue that informal workers are likely to work under worse working conditions and lack social protection that may produce a devastating "snowball" effect which, in its turn, may negatively affect economic agents' working life, housing quality, poverty, and their physical and mental health.

Chrenekova et al. (2016) investigated the relationship between informal employment and quality of life in Ukraine. In their research, the latter variable was represented by average monthly wage PPP and unemployment rate to quality as the objective dimension, and self-perception of households of their income and material welfare to quantify as the subjective dimension. The empirical results revealed the statistically significant differences in the size of informal employment in rural and urban areas: a significantly larger share of informal employment – as much as 79.9% – is recorded in rural areas where the largest share of informal workers are involved in agriculture, forestry, and farming. A relatively unfavorable relationship between informal employment and quality of life was identified by both the objective and subjective dimensions of the analysis. The largest share of informally operating economic agents perceive the economic situation of their household as poor (with low disposable income) and say they cannot afford even the most important items in the consumer basket. Even when the level of informal employment in rural areas is growing, population's income level is not increasing, but decreasing significantly. Thus, even the ability of a rural area to create informal jobs, which is confirmed by empirical results, does not increase population's material well-being, and thus the quality of life. These findings are in line with the results provided by Cuevas et al. (2009) who indicate that economic agents operating in the informal sector get low pay or are unpaid, and the mean monthly income of workers in the informal group is relatively lower than that of workers in the mixed (i.e., working both formally and informally) group.

Alvarez et al.'s (2016) research, aimed at identifying the relationship between elderly people's informal employment and quality of life, disclosed that the respondents favorably perceive various dimensions of quality of life, primarily health. This positive perception is linked to increased activity, good physical and mental health, finding meaning in life, making stronger social contacts, and productive aging.

Kireenko and Nevzorova (2015) conducted a comprehensive study of the relationship between the informal economy and quality of life based on the original sample of 150 countries. Their study was based on the presumption that while informal activities may raise the overall income of the population, they may negatively affect other indicators of quality of life, and through them may have a negative impact on the overall quality of life. The authors found that life expectancy at birth and children in-school rate indicators were statistically significant in the analyzed sample. The results also disclosed that when the size of the informal economy is rising, the quality of life is also rising, but at the same time the indicators of a long and healthy life and access to knowledge are decreasing.

Pfau-Effinger's (2017) research in Moldova revealed that one of the main reasons why economic agents get involved in informal employment is a lack of alternatives in the labor market, particularly in rural areas. Nevertheless, even operating in the informal sector does not raise economic agents' quality of life because, as the empirical results indicate, informal employment is related to a low level of education and limited social benefits (unemployment benefits, pensions).

Rojas (2013) analyzed the relationship between informal employment and quality of life, represented by economic agents' life satisfaction, job satisfaction, satisfaction with some job-related attributes, satisfaction in other domains of life, and experiences of well-being. The research disclosed that the difference between subjective well-being, perceived by either formal or informal workers is very little, which proposes that, compared with formal employment, informal employment is not associated with either a better or worse quality of life. The opposite results were obtained by Pourreza et al. (2018) who surveyed 112 formally employed and the same number of informally employed randomly selected women representing Iranian society. The results disclosed that the mean score of the quality of life estimated for the women employed in the formal sector was significantly higher than that estimated for the women employed in the informal sector. In addition, it was found that almost half of women working in the informal sector do not have a high school diploma, suggesting that informal employment may be linked to the low level of education of informal economic operators. The lack of social security and inadequate wages were identified as the main social problems faced in the informal sector.

According to Lehmann and Pignatti (2018), when economic agents are pushed into the informal sector against their will (i.e., when the labor market is segmented), their well-being and quality of life decline, but when economic agents are free to choose to operate in the informal sector (i.e., when the labor market is integrated), their well-being and quality of life can reach a much higher level. The authors also note that most informal economic agents engage in informal employment involuntarily and use it as a waiting stage to enter formal salaried employment. Nevertheless, their empirical results for the Ukrainian labor market are mixed, which suggests that informal work is not always associated with lower quality of life and reduced well-being.

The impact of the labor market segmentation/integration aspect was also confirmed by Bertranou et al. (2014). The authors analyzed the segmentation phenomenon in Argentina by invoking the employment mobility factor and researched the potential sub-segments that are likely to exist within formal salaried employment, informal salaried employment, and self-employment. Their findings indicate that the level and nature of informal employment in Argentina is determined not by a single cause (i.e., explicit exclusion or escape in the form of self-realization), but a variety of factors. The research disclosed that the governmental regulatory policies aimed at deregulation, greater labor market flexibility, and reduction in the cost of labor (specifically, through reducing social security contributions) do not necessarily lead to a resounding drop in informal employment because they contribute to raising job quality, and at the same time quality of life in the informal sector. Although the informal self-employed are excluded from both the formal sector of the economy and salaried employment, informal employment is still preferable.

In conclusion, informal employment is not always associated with either a better or worse quality of life compared with formal employment. Literature analysis indicates that although informal employment can provide relatively good economic benefits, social connections, and the feeling of satisfaction, informally operating economic agents often face the problems of occupational safety and health (both physical and mental), they may have limited access to knowledge and in most cases lack social security coverage. It is interesting to note that job and life quality of the self-employed operating in the informal sector can be promoted by regulatory simplification, greater labor market flexibility and reduction in the cost of labor, although these measures are commonly considered to prompt informal workers to return to the formal sector of the economy.

2.6 The Nature of the Relationship Between Unemployment and the Informal Economy

The relationship between unemployment and the informal economy remains one of the most popularly discussed issues and lies at the heart of much policy making. In popular culture, there is often a perception that it is the unemployed who engage in the informal economy, sometimes when claiming state benefits, and that action is required to tackle this phenomenon. Policymakers, meanwhile, seek to understand the nature of this relationship to develop the targeted measures to reduce unemployment and the size of the informal economy. For researchers, interest in this relationship arises because previous studies have not yet provided convincing evidence as to whether the relationship is positive, negative, or not significant. Indeed, although the literature is rich in studies focused on the causal relationship between unemployment and the informal economy, the results of previous studies on the direction of this relationship are multifarious.

Giles and Tedds (2002) argue that the relationship between unemployment and the informal economy is conditioned by two opposing forces. On the one hand, a decrease in the size of the informal economy can be caused by an increase in the unemployment rate because the level of the informal economy is positively correlated with the GDP growth rate (Okun's law). This means that since the size of the informal economy is positively related to GDP growth rate, which, in its turn, is negatively correlated with the unemployment rate, the growing total number of the unemployed may also statistically reduce the number of people working in the informal sector, thus reducing the statistical size of the informal economy. On the other hand, rising unemployment rates can push the unemployed to act in the informal sector both because it is one of the means of earning income and because the unemployed have more time to organize and conduct this type of activity than the employed (Alexandru, 2013).

The above-presented literature analysis reveals the heterogeneous nature of the determinants and forms of operating in the informal economy and the informal labor market which, in its turn, causes heterogeneity of the relationship between unemployment and the informal economy. Table 2.6 provides a summary review of some previous findings on the nature of the relationship between unemployment and the informal economy.

The information provided in Table 2.6 shows that vast majority of previous studies on the relationship between the unemployment rate and the informal economy confirm the existence of the relationship between the phenomena under consideration, but the findings concerning the direction and intensity of this relationship

Table 2.6 Review of some previous findings on the nature of the relationship between unemployment and the informal economy

Author(s), year	Research method(s)	Research sample, period	Findings
The studies that confirm the positive relationship between unemployment rate and the informal economy			
Davidescu and Dobre (2012)	A Tado-Yamamoto approach	USA, 1980–2009	The relationship between the variables is positive, unidirectional
Dell'Anno and Solomon (2008)	SVAR analysis	The USA, 1970–2004	The relationship between the variables is positive in the short run
Abada et al. (2021)	The Tado-Yamamoto approach, the Modified Wald (MWald) test	Nigeria, 1980:Q1-2018:Q4	The relationship between the variables is strong, positive and unidirectional
Manes et al. (2016)	Advanced dynamic panel techniques, error correction models	47 countries, 1991–2014	The relationship between the variables is positive, and they are bound to long-term equilibrium
Dobre and Alexandru (2009)	The structural equation model (SEM)	Spain, 1970–2007	The relationship between the informal economy and the unemployment rate is positive
Hasanvand et al. (2016)	System Generalized Method of Moments (System GMM) approach.	67 developing countries, 1999–2009	The unemployment rate has a positive effect on the informal economy
Alexandru et al. (2010)	Johansen and Granger approaches for cointegration, the MIMIC	USA, 1980–2009	The relationship is strong and unidirectional in the long run
Bajada and Schneider (2009)	The MIMIC	12 OECD countries, 1991–2005	Due to the substitution effect, the unemployment rate fluctuation (whether positive or negative) has a similar impact on the informal economy fluctuations in the short run
The studies that confirm the negative relationship between unemployment rate and the informal economy			
Sahnoun and Abdennadher (2019)	A dynamic simultaneous-equation panel data model	38 developing and 40 developed countries, 2000–2015	The relationship between the variables is negative and bidirectional or unidirectional in developed or developing economies respectively

(continued)

Table 2.6 (continued)

Author(s), year	Research method(s)	Research sample, period	Findings
Giles and Tedds (2002)	Two-way Granger causality	Canada, 1976–1995	The unemployment rate negatively correlates with the informal economy; the relationship between the variables is weak
The studies that confirm the neutral relationship between unemployment rate and the informal economy			
Saafi et al. (2015)	Threshold cointegration approach and Kyrtsou and Labys's nonlinear causality test	32 developed and developing countries, 1980–2009	The relationship between the variables is neutral, bidirectional or unidirectional
The studies that provide mixed results			
Abdlaziz et al. (2020)	The Toda-Yamamoto causality approach and panel Granger causality test	Selected Middle East and North African countries, 1991–2015	The relationship between the variables can be unidirectional or bidirectional, depending on a country
Davidescu (2014)	ARDL, SVAR methods	Romania, 2000–2013	The relationship between the variables may vary depending on a period, research method and measurement of the variables

Source: compiled by the authors

significantly vary, particularly in the context of developed and developing economies. It is also not always clear whether the relationship is temporary or permanent.

Several studies provide the robust finding that the relationship between the unemployment rate and the informal economy is ***positive.*** These studies support the view that under the conditions of the aggregate supply and the labor market shock, the informal economy acts as a buffer and absorbs a proportion of the workers who have lost their jobs with a decrease in the number of workplaces in the formal economy and who have started operating in the informal sector.

In Mauleon and Sarda's (2017) research, the size of the informal economy is estimated as a direct function of the tax and unemployment rates. The relationship between the variables was found to be extremely strong in the countries that are characterized by high unemployment rates (e.g., Spain, Greece) and less strong in the countries characterized by moderate unemployment rates (e.g., Italy, Germany). The unemployment rate was found to have a strong significant impact on the size of the informal economy during periods of economic downturn (e.g., in 2008). Davidescu and Dobre (2012) employed the Toda-Yamamoto method for researching the relationship between the unemployment rate and the size of the informal economy in the USA over the 1980–2009 period and found a unidirectional causality running from the former to the latter variable. The size of the informal economy was also found to be significantly caused by taxes on corporate income, social insurance contributions and self-employment.

When examining how the size of the informal economy responds to an aggregate supply shock, Dell'Anno and Solomon (2008) found that the relationship between unemployment rate and the informal economy is positive in the short run (the authors analyzed the situation in the USA over the 1970–2004 period by employing SVAR analysis). In this case, an aggregate supply shock was selected to represent a temporary shock in unemployment, and the research revealed that a positive aggregate supply shock causes the informal economy to rise about 8%.

In Abada et al.'s (2021) research, the unemployment rate was identified to be one of the four multiple causes of the informal economy in Nigeria (along with the tax burden, self-employment and governmental social benefits). Similar results were obtained by Ogbuabor and Malaolu (2013) who found the unemployment rate to be one of the major drivers of the informal economy along with the tax burden, governmental regulation, and inflation. The positive effect that the unemployment rate has on the informal economy in 67 developing economies was also confirmed in Hasanvand et al.'s (2016) study. Abada et al.'s (2021) research revealed the existence of a strong and positive relationship between the unemployment rate and the informal economy, which was confirmed by the coefficient of determination equal to 0.89. Application of the Tado-Yamamoto methodology and the Modified Wald (MWald) test disclosed that a unidirectional causality runs from unemployment rate to the size of the informal economy at a 1% significance level.

Manes et al. (2016) employed a simple job search model which assumed that the return on informal activities tends to decline, and informal operators undergo the negative congestion effects in job searching. The authors found a long-term equilibrium relationship between unemployment and the informal economy, *ceteris paribus*. They argue that the long-term impact of unemployment on the informal economy is much smaller in the countries with less stringent labor market regulation, but even in this case the relationship between the variables in question remains positive and statistically significant. The research also disclosed that the rate of return to long-term equilibrium after a temporary economic shock is three times higher in the countries with less stringent labor market regulation than in the countries with stringent regulation. On the one hand, these results suggest that the growth in the size of the informal economy is limited because informally active workers eventually return to the formal labor market. On the other hand, the results reveal the dependence of the level of informal work on labor market regulation. The more stringently regulated is the labor market, the more difficult it is for informal workers to return to the formal sector.

It should be noted that the results obtained in some previous studies indicate a potential variation in the direction of the relationship between the variables in the short and long run. For instance, Alexandru (2013) analyzed the relationship between unemployment rate and the informal economy in Romania over the 2000Q1–2010Q2 period by employing the bounds test within the ARDL modeling approach (the former variable was represented by the ILO unemployment rate and registered unemployment rate, while the latter was represented by % of official

GDP obtained by currency demand approach). The empirical results indicate that both the ILO and registered unemployment rates have *negative* statistically significant effects on the informal economy in the short run, while their long-run effects on the informal economy are *positive.* Expressed as a percentage, a 1% increase in the registered unemployment rate leads to an average increase of 0.40% in the size of the informal economy, while a 1% increase in the unemployment rate estimated by the ILO leads to an average increase of 2.17% in the size of the informal economy. The empirical application of the ARDL causality test disclosed a long-run unidirectional causality running from both the above-mentioned unemployment rates to the informal economy. The short-run causality running from registered unemployment rate to the informal economy was confirmed by the significance of F-statistic value. The negative short-run effects can be explained by inability of the labor market to provide enough workplaces under the conditions when unemployment rate is rising, that is, by the limited employment potential in the informal sector. However, if the unemployment rate is rising in the long run, the unemployed have enough time to adapt and find employment niches, so the rise in the unemployment rate leads to an expansion of the informal economy (positive effects). These results are in line with Alexandru et al.'s (2010) findings, which confirm a unidirectional causality running from the unemployment rate to the informal economy, and Bajada and Schneider's (2009) empirical results, according to which short-run fluctuations in the unemployment rate have a direct impact on short-run fluctuations in the informal economy, although the probability of the long-run causality running from unemployment to the informal economy is not excluded.

In their later studies, Davidescu and Dobre (2013) analyzed the relationship between the variables in the USA over the 1982–2011 period by applying the structural VAR method and found the positive relationship between the variables in the short run, but the long-run relationship was not confirmed. Davidescu (2014) employed the ARDL and SVAR methods to research the relationship between the variables in Romania over the 2000–2013 period. The empirical results of the ARDL analysis did not reveal any long-run relationship between the unemployment rate and the informal economy in the country under consideration, while the findings of the SVAR analysis propose that the growing recorded unemployment rate causes the size of the informal economy to rise in the short run. Interestingly, the results of the SVAR analysis revealed that the rising ILO unemployment rate leads to a decrease in the size of the informal economy.

Abdlaziz et al.'s (2020) research of the situation in the selected MENA countries over the 1991–2015 period, based on the Toda-Yamamoto causality, delivered mixed results. A unidirectional causality running from the informal economy to unemployment rate was identified for Bahrain, Jordan, and Lebanon, but a unidirectional causality running from the unemployment rate to the informal economy was identified for Turkey and Qatar. The bidirectional causality was identified for Algeria only. The panel Granger causality test revealed the bidirectional causality between the variables for the MENA region, but only with consideration of one and three lags. With consideration of two, four, and five lags, a unidirectional causality running from the informal economy to the unemployment rate was identified.

The empirical results, which show variations in the relationship between unemployment rate and the informal economy depending on the period under consideration, the target country(ies), the method selected for measuring unemployment rate and/or the size of the informal economy, the lag factor and other determinants, confirm Dell'Anno et al.'s (2007) assertion. This proposes that if the theory of economics does not provide any clear unanimous evidence to indicate whether the sign of the relationship between unemployment rate and the informal economy is positive or negative, it is presumed that the causal relationship between these variables is positive.

Nevertheless, other empirical results contradict this view and confirm the ***negative*** relationship between the unemployment rate and the informal economy. A negative correlation between the variables was found by Giles and Tedds (2002), whose results additionally indicate that the relationship between the variables is weak. The authors explain the weakness of the relationship by the fact that in some cases an increase in the unemployment rate may simply coincide with a decrease in the informal economy but given the number of the unemployed in the informal sector, this situation can statistically increase the size of the informal economy. Based on the results of their study, Giles and Tedds (2002) conclude that no net effects that the unemployment rate has on the scope of the informal economy are statistically significant. In terms of the negative relationship between the variables under consideration, Kolm and Larsen (2003) argue that the size of the informal economy can decline, and the official employment rate can increase significantly if the national government undertakes target measures of stricter control (e.g., imposes stricter penalties for informal activities), but this is not related to a reduction in the unemployment rate. According to the authors, it is more severe penalties (especially fines) that stimulate the demand for officially earned wages because the risk of informal economic activities becomes associated with excessive risk costs.

Sahnoun and Abdennadher's (2019) research revealed the negative and bidirectional causality between the unemployment rate and the informal economy in developed economies, while developing economies were confirmed to have the negative, but unidirectional causality running from the unemployment rate to the informal economy. The strength of the relationship between the variables under consideration was found to be significantly affected by institutional quality. Namely, the countries characterized by high institutional quality tended to have their unemployment rate weaker affecting the size of the informal economy, while the countries characterized by low institutional quality demonstrated their unemployment rate stronger affecting the size of the informal economy.

Finally, the third group of studies cover those that disclose a ***neutral*** relationship between the unemployment rate and the informal economy. Saafi et al. (2015) empirically investigated the dynamic relationship between unemployment and the informal economy in 32 developed and developing countries over the 1980–2009 period by employing the threshold cointegration approach and Kyrtsou and Labys's (2006) nonlinear causality test. The results revealed the neutral relationship between the variables under consideration in some countries in the sample (Bolivia, China, Colombia, Pakistan, the Philippines and Portugal), but these findings were not supported for the rest of the sample. The relationship was confirmed to be bidirectional in Finland and Sweden, which proposes that high unemployment rates lead to a larger size of the informal economy, and vice versa. The relationship was confirmed to be unidirectional (i.e., running from unemployment to the informal economy) in Jamaica, the USA, and Venezuela, which leads to the conclusion that a faster growth of the unemployment rate may lead to a faster growth of the size of the informal economy. On the contrary, the relationship between the variables was confirmed to be unidirectional but running from the informal economy to the unemployment rate in Chile.

In conclusion, although vast majority of previous studies confirm the existence of a positive relationship between the unemployment rate and the informal economy and only a small number of studies provide empirical evidence that this relationship can be negative or neutral, it is not always clear whether the relationship is temporary or permanent in nature. The strength and direction of the relationship between the unemployment rate and the informal economy can be determined by the target period (short or long run, a phase of an economic cycle – a period of an economic upswing or recession), the method selected for measuring unemployment rate and/or the size of the informal economy, the lag factor, and other determinants. In addition, the direction and intensity of this relationship may significantly vary in the context of developed and developing economies. As noted by Sahnoun and Abdennadher (2019), the level of national economic development can significantly affect the intensity and the direction of the causality between the unemployment rate and the informal economy because in contrast to economic operators acting in developing economies, the ones acting in the informal sector of developed economies can have less internal incentives or external opportunities to operate informally. All of this indicates that although there is quite a lot of studies focused on the issue under consideration, the general understanding of the interdependence between the unemployment rate and the informal economy is still limited. It is for this reason that the rest of this book reports a study that examines this issue in Lithuania.

Chapter 3
Relationship Between Unemployment and the Informal Economy in Lithuania

To report the study on the relationship between unemployment and the informal economy in Lithuania, the first section reviews the materials and methods used, while the second section reports the findings regarding both the characteristics of the unemployed and their motivations for participating in the informal economy.

3.1 Materials and Methods

Representative surveys are often employed to investigate the informal economy and the informal labor market. Thus, to fulfill the empirical purpose of this research – to identify the relationship between unemployment and the informal economy in Lithuanian municipalities – representative surveys were employed. The surveys were based on the quantitative research method. The respondents were delivered a survey link online. When answering the questions, the respondents had multiple response options (see the questionnaire in Annex 2). The survey population consisted of persons of working age (18–65 years of age) who were unemployed at the time of the survey. A total of 1047 surveys were conducted. The respondents represented 60 Lithuanian municipalities. To ensure the appropriate representativeness of the survey, the number of the respondents representing each municipality was estimated based on the number of the unemployed in each municipality. The research was conducted over the period November–December 2020.

Expert evaluation is the second method selected to conduct research on the relationship between unemployment rate and the informal economy (see Annex 3). Selection of this method was based on the two following factors: first, the lack of the primary statistical information on the issue under consideration; and second, the representatives of municipalities are best acquainted with the labor market problems in their respective municipality.

L. Gasparėnienė et al., *Unemployment and the Informal Economy*, SpringerBriefs in Economics, https://doi.org/10.1007/978-3-030-96687-4_3

Depending on the research purpose and the competence of the experts in the area under consideration, an expert evaluation should involve 10–100 experts. Meanwhile, according to Augustinaitis et al. (2009), to ensure the accuracy and reliability of an expert evaluation, an expert group should consist of at least five experts. The expert evaluation was carried out indirectly based on a pre-designed questionnaire. The experts were delivered a survey link online. In addition to highlighting creativity, approach to expertise, flexibility of thinking, reliability, self-criticism and other qualities an expert must possess, the literature places particular emphasis on *the expert competence* (Augustinaitis et al., 2009). Thus, when selecting the experts, the researchers focused on the expert competence, work experience in the activity area, and the knowledge about the situation of (un)employment and the informal economy in Lithuania. Based on the above-mentioned criteria, 219 persons responded in the expert group (300 questionnaires were sent out, 219 were returned). Distribution of the experts by the position they hold is depicted in Fig. 3.1.

Analysis and interpretation of the results. The questionnaire for experts consisted of two parts. The first part was intended to collect the general information about an expert (municipality and the work area). The second part was intended to find out an expert's opinion about the causal and consequential factors determining involvement of the unemployed in the informal economy. The latter part of the questionnaire serves as a basis for identifying the determinants of operation of the unemployed in the informal labor market and developing the recommendations to the relevant state institutions.

The respondents selected as experts were asked to rate each statement on a scale from 1 to 4 (from the numerical value 1 representing the meaning "I completely disagree/It is completely insignificant" to the numerical value 4 representing the meaning "I completely agree/It is completely significant"). A rank lower than 2.5 or

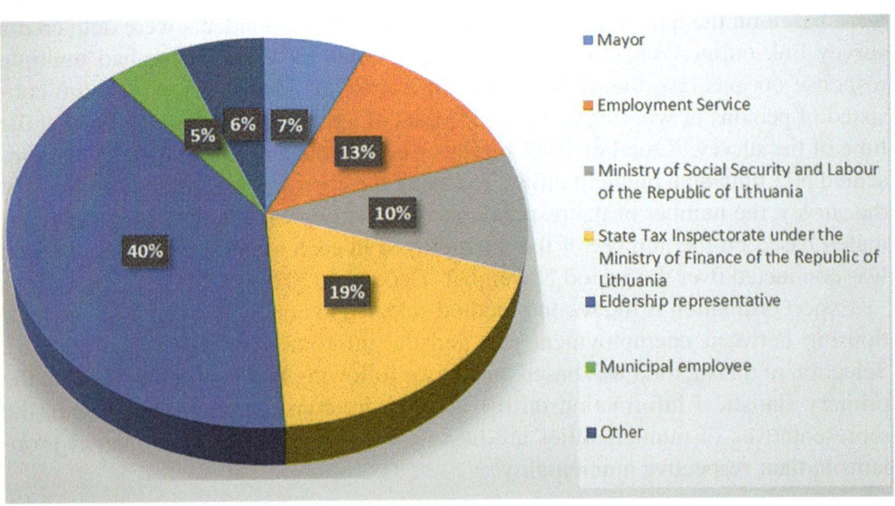

Fig. 3.1 Distribution of the experts by the position, percent (compiled by the authors based on the research results)

equal to 2.5 indicated that a factor was considered insignificant, while the rank higher than 2.5 indicated that a factor was considered significant. The results of the expert evaluation were processed by employing the SPSS (*"Statistical Package for Social Sciences"*) and "Microsoft Excel" software. The numerical values of the ranks were transferred to a special ranking table (see Table 3.1).

Value V_{jn} in Table 3.1 indicates the significance level at which the *j*th expert rated the *n*th statement in the questionnaire. The obtained data are systematized, the rank sum $\mathbf{V}_i$ for the *i*th statement is calculated, the mean $\overline{s}$ of the rank sum $\mathbf{S}_i$ for the *i*th statement is derived, the significance of each statement is estimated, and Kendall's coefficient of concordance *W*, representing consistency of the experts' opinions, is found. Kendall's coefficient of concordance may vary in the interval $0 \leq W \leq 1$. The value of the coefficient closer to 1 indicates more consistent opinions of the experts. If $W \leq 0.6$, it is considered that consistency of the expert evaluations is weak, but if $p < 0.05$, then the data are reliably consistent.

When providing the results of the expert evaluation, particular attention should be paid to the interpretation of the *Cronbach's alpha* coefficient. Some researchers, for instance, Nunnally and Bernstein (1994), state that the *Cronbach's alpha* should be no lower than 0.7, while some other researchers say that the critical cut-off for reliability of a questionnaire is 0.6. Selection of the critical cut-off is a subjective matter which may also depend on the nature and qualitative aspects of a particular study. 0.6 was selected to represent the lowest value of the *Cronbach's alpha* for this empirical research. Furthermore, in our study, we provide a detailed description of the empirical research stages that will help to fulfill the intended purpose.

To verify the relationship between unemployment rate and the size of the informal economy in Lithuanian municipalities over the 2001–2019 period, the classical Pearson correlation matrix and the robust Minimum Covariance Determinant (MCD) correlation matrix were employed.

Table 3.1 Matrix of the results of the expert evaluation representing the causal and consequential factors of involvement of the unemployed in the informal sector and providing grounds for recommendations to the relevant institutions on how to improve the employment situation

	Factors (V)					
Experts	1	2	…	i	…	N
1	V_{11}	V_{12}	…	V_{1i}	…	V_{1n}
2	V_{21}	V_{22}	…	V_{2i}	…	V_{2n}
…	…	…	…	…	…	…
J	V_{j1}	V_{j2}	…	V_{ji}	…	V_{jn}
…	…	…	…	…	…	…
M	V_{m1}	V_{m2}	…	V_{mi}	…	V_{mn}
Rank sum						
Kendall's coefficient of concordance, *W*						
p-value						
Frequency of the attribute indication						

Source: Augustinaitis et al. (2009)

In the first stage of the empirical calculations, the informal economy was explained through the MIMIC model by using the data of 60 municipalities for the period between 2001 and 2019. The entire period under consideration was divided into such sub-periods as a pre-crisis sub-period (2001–2007), a crisis sub-period (2008–2010), and a post-crisis sub-period (2011–2019), which were examined in detail. At the end of this examination, immigration and employment were found to be the most important variables affecting the size of the informal economy (see Annex 4).

The relationship between the size of the informal economy (% of GDP) and the unemployment rate in each municipality was examined by invoking the method of correlation analysis which was based on the classical Pearson correlation matrix and the robust Minimum Covariance Determinant (MCD) correlation matrix. The MCD correlation matrix is a matrix that does not lose its ability to represent the data even if any extraneous factors are observed in the data set and is resistant to the influence of external observations.

The MCD correlation matrix is based on an algorithm involving different levers of extraneous phenomena (Hubert & Debruyne, 2010). The MCD method was proposed by Rousseeuw (1984), and later an improved algorithm was introduced by Rousseeuw and Van Driessen (1999). It is widely used to identify extraneous observations in a dataset. This method is aimed at identifying h observations (from the total number n), the covariance matrix of which has the smallest determinant. To identify the most homogeneous group of observations, the MCD algorithm employs the Mahalonobi distance method.

3.2 Findings

For those who use proxy indirect measures of the informal economy, rather than conduct direct surveys of respondents, the common argument is that this is justified because respondents will be unwilling to report their informal economic activities to researchers. However, the important initial finding of this survey was that respondents openly expressed their views on the informal economy and there appeared to be little reticence in answering the questions put to them. This provides a justification in future studies to use direct survey methods when seeking to understand participation in the informal economy. As

To analyze the results, firstly, the level of participation of the unemployed in the informal economy in Lithuania is reported from both the supply and demand sides. Secondly, the reasons for participation in the informal economy are reported by the respondents, and thirdly and finally, the relationship between the unemployment rate and the informal economy in municipalities.

3.2.1 *Level of Participation of the Unemployed in the Informal Economy*

To evaluate the level of participation in the informal economy of the unemployed, both the demand and supply sides are here analyzed.

3.2.1.1 Purchase of Goods and Services from the Informal Economy

Starting with the demand side, the respondents were also asked if over the period of the last 12 months they had paid for any goods or services realizing that the income earned from these goods or services was not likely to be declared (e.g., no receipt or VAT invoice was issued). The finding is that 70% of the unemployed have bought goods or services being aware that the income earned from these products and services is not declared. Of the remainder, 24% state that they have not done so, and 3% have done unintentionally not being aware at the time of purchase that the income would be concealed. Figure 3.2 examines the type goods or services purchased where it was realized that the income earned from these goods or services was not likely to be declared.

Over one-third (36%) of all goods and services purchased on a non-declared basis were in the health care sector. In the health care sector, these informal payments involve an exchange, in cash or in kind, in which the health care employees and patients are involved, so that the latter benefit from certain services, which otherwise should have been offered free of charge in the public sector (Balabanova

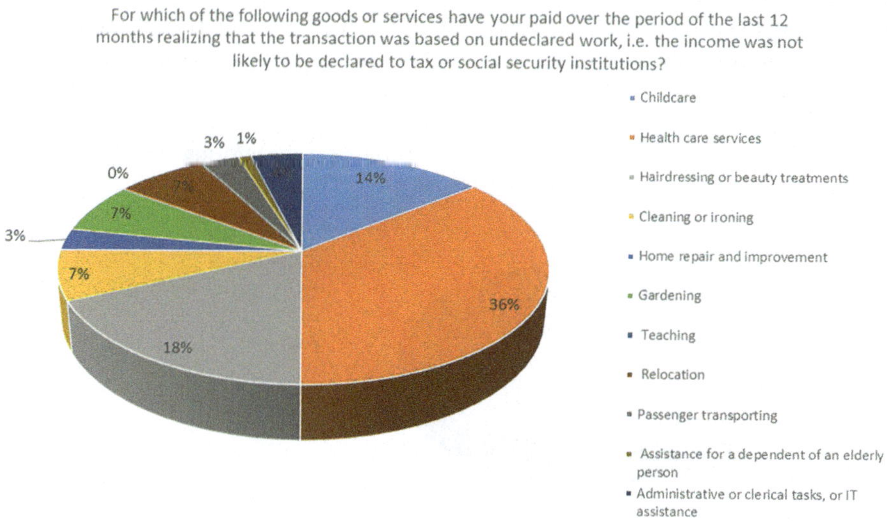

Fig. 3.2 Goods and services purchased in the informal economy

& McKee, 2002). The requests for informal payments can be initiated by doctors, such as when they consider that their salaries are low (Jaminson et al., 2006) or by patients who consider that they will receive better care (Gaal et al., 2006). If the patient offers the informal payment, it is often seen as a "gift" while if the health care staff request it, such informal payments are more of a "bribe." These informal payments are known by many different names including: "bribes/bribe payments"; "envelope payments"; "gratitude payments"; "informal payments"; "red packages/ envelope"; "under-the-table payments"; and "unofficial payments/fees" (Chereches et al., 2013).

Given that this survey was conducted in November–December 2020 and the purchasers were asked about the last 12 months, much of this period covers the time of the COVID-19 pandemic and the informal payments will be related to this pandemic. These informal payments will therefore be payments to gain preferential access to health care services associated with the pandemic.

Beyond the health care sector, 18% of purchases of goods and services from the informal economy in the realm of hairdressing and other beauty treatments. This again could well be associated with the pandemic since during lockdown, access to formal economy services were limited. During these lockdown periods, therefore, hairdressing and beauty treatments would have been by necessity accessed in the informal economy since there would have been no access to formal economy providers. A further 14% of purchases from the informal economy had been for childcare services, with the remainder for cleaning and ironing services (7% of all purchases in the informal economy), gardening services (7%), help moving home/ relocation services (7%), and teaching services (3%).

It is often assumed that the only reason that consumers purchase goods and services in the informal economy is due to the lower cost. In other words, it is seen as a way of saving money. This can be assumed to be even more likely to be the rationale among the unemployed. However, Fig. 3.3 reveals that just 59% of respondents purchase undeclared goods or services only because of a lower price. This is in line

Fig. 3.3 The reasons for purchasing informal goods/services, percent

with previous research. Lower price does not represent the only valid explanation for consumers engaging in the informal economy. For example, a study across 11 Central and Eastern European Countries finds that the lower cost justification alone is the reason for only 30% of informal purchases (Williams & Horodnic, 2016). This relates to a representative sample of all consumers, rather than solely the unemployed which is the case in this study).

What other reasons exist, therefore, for purchasing goods and services from the informal economy? Over the past decade or so, the view of consumers as rational economic actors whose behavior is governed by financial gain has been transcended. A social actor theoretical perspective has been adopted in relation to the demand side of the informal economy. This asserts that a significant number of transactions of goods and services in the informal economy involve kin, acquaintances, neighbors, friends or work colleagues. For example, one might pay close social relations for goods or services (i.e., babysitting, house cleaning) to consolidate the relationship or to help them if in need of money, as providing money for a service does not conjure up any notion of charity, which might lead them to refuse the money. Therefore, from this social actor perspective, informal transactions are seen as a form of community exchange or active citizenship grounded in notions of mutual aid and reciprocity (Williams, 2008). Therefore, consumers choose to buy products or services from the informal market to strengthen their social relations.

This social actor perspective is reinforced in this study of the unemployed in Lithuania. A total of 15% of the purchases in the informal economy were made for mainly reasons associated with this social actor theoretical perspective, 8% of purchases were made with the intention of helping somebody who needed money, and 7% of purchases as favor to friends, relatives, or colleagues. Again, this is in line with previous studies. For example, a study across 11 Central and Eastern European Countries finds that the social actor justification is the main reason for 13% of informal purchases (Williams & Horodnic, 2016).

Besides these rational economic actor and social actor explanations, a final theoretical perspective has argued that purchases in the informal economy occur due to the failures of the formal economy in delivering goods and services to citizens in terms of the lack of availability, speed, and quality of the formal economy (Williams, 2008; Williams & Horodnic, 2016). This is reinforced in this study of Lithuania. It has been found that customers choose to buy informal goods and services due to formal provision being poorer in terms of speed of provision (10% of the consumers), quality of provision (10% of the consumers), or even due to the lack of availability of the wanted good or service on the formal market (3% of consumers). Again, this is in line with a previous study across 11 Central and Eastern European Countries (Williams & Horodnic, 2016).

While the three above theoretical perspectives imply that the consumer is aware that they participate in the informal market and do so voluntarily, it cannot be asserted that all purchases from the informal economy are made knowingly by consumers. The consumer might also participate in the informal economy because they are unaware that their transaction is informal until after the purchase has been made and they did not receive a receipt or an invoice. In this study of Lithuania, the finding is that 3% of purchases in the informal economy are made unintentionally. This is supported by previous recent research on the European home repairs and renovation sector, which finds that 4% of the purchases are made unintentionally, the consumer realizing only after the purchase has been made (Williams & Kosta, 2020, 2021).

3.2.1.2 Supply Side: Participation of the Unemployed in the Informal Economy

To examine the level of participation of the unemployed in the informal economy, the unemployed respondents were first asked about whether they knew others who work informally. This enabled a gradual approach to asking them directly whether they engaged themselves in such work which previous studies reveal is an effective way of designing surveys to elicit responses. The finding was that 92% of the unemployed know about one or more persons working informally. Of all respondents who were if they personally know any people who work without declaring all or a part of their income to social security institutions, more than half (56%) of the respondents know 1–2 people, and more than a third (36%) know 2 or more people. Just 8% did not know anybody who worked informally. This displays the embeddedness of informality as a perceived social norm.

Turning to whether they had engaged in informal work, 68% of the unemployed respondents have received unofficial income. The remaining 32% has not operated in the informal labor market while unemployed. This reveals, therefore, the prevalence of participation in the informal economy among the unemployed in Lithuania.

Examining the type of informal work in which they engaged, most had engaged in housekeeping, construction, and/or agricultural work. That is, 40% of those participating in the informal economy had engaged in housecleaning, 21% in construction work, 23% worked in the agricultural sector, and 8% provided repair services, 4% provided beauty services, and 4% childcare services.

Indeed, examining whether they view engaging in informal work as acceptable, the finding was that 62% of all respondents indicate that they view participation in informal economic activities as acceptable, providing further support for the view that informality is perceived as a socially legitimate activity in Lithuania. Breaking this down to see if some types of informal work are viewed as more acceptable to engage in than others, the finding is that this is not necessarily the case. That is, 43% of the respondents find acceptable income non-declaring when an individual person or a self-employed evades taxes by hiding all or a part of one's income, 41% of the respondents find acceptable income non-declaring when a firm hires an individual person and pays a part of the wages informally ("envelope wages"), 38% find it acceptable when a firm hires another firm and business activities are not declared to the authorities, 36% find it acceptable when a business is hired by a private household and the income is not declared to the tax and social security authorities, and 29% find it acceptable when a private person is hired by another household and the income is not declared to the authorities.

Moreover, 75% of the respondents see no reason why they should not accept undeclared income from an employer. Of all respondents, 49% would any amount and 26% only small amounts. Just 25% would not accept such undeclared income from an employer. Turning to whether this has occurred in practice when they had been working, 30% of all respondents had accepted undeclared income from an employer, and only 17% had refused such income. The remaining 53% stated that they did not know.

As such, this survey reveals that over two-thirds (68%) of the unemployed respondents had worked in the informal economy while they were unemployed. How, therefore, can this participation in the informal economy be explained?

3.2.2 Motives for Participation in the Informal Economy

Both the unemployed and the experts were asked to rank the causes of unemployment in the context of the presence of an informal economy by their significance. The experts indicated the following main causes of unemployment (see Table 3.2). The value of *the Cronbach's alpha* for the questionnaire was equal to 0.746; p = 0.000. According to the experts, the potential not to declare one's income and at the same time receive unemployment benefits is one of the main determinants of unemployment. This is followed by insufficiently high wages in the region leading to the amount of the social benefits demotivating the unemployed to search for a paid job. This factor was indicated as the major reason why the unemployed tend to constantly look for a job.

Turning to the main reasons for unemployment in the context of the presence of an informal economy from the point of view of the unemployed themselves, the main reasons are insufficiently high wages in the positions offered and that they live

Table 3.2 The causes of unemployment (the results of the expert evaluation)

No.	Causal factors	Mean value	Mode[a]	Min value	Max value
1.	Living on the benefit, an unemployed selects cheaper smuggled goods	3.23	3	1	4
2.	Wages in regions are insufficiently high; as a result, the amount of social benefits demotivates the unemployed to search for a paid job	3.36	3	1	4
3.	Justification of informal activities when purchasing undeclared goods/services	3.05	3	1	4
4.	***The potential not to declare income and at the same time receive unemployment benefits***	***3.46***	***4***	***2***	***4***
5.	Prolonged operation without declaring one's income caused by long-term unemployment	3.23	3	2	4
6.	Lack of public awareness	3.21	3	1	4

Source: compiled by the authors based on the results of the expert evaluation
[a]The most common value

in a region with a high unemployment rate and they are excluded when particular job positions require travel to larger cities because they cannot travel (Table 3.3).

When analyzing the consequences of unemployment from the experts' point of view (see Table 3.4), the informal economy was asserted by them to mainly affect the official long-term unemployed, when income is earned in the informal labor market and is not declared (mean value is equal to 3.41).

To tackle participation in the informal economy, two contrasting policy approaches have been adopted, each of which seek to tackle different causes. The first approach assumes that those engaged in the informal economy are rational economic actors who weigh up the costs and benefits of participating in the informal economy, and if the expected benefits outweigh the costs, then they participate. This rational economic actor theory, rooted historically in the work of Jeremy Bentham, was developed and applied to the informal economy in the early 1970s by Allingham and Sandmo (1972). They asserted that if state authorities are to ensure that the costs outweigh the benefits, then there is a need to focus upon increasing the costs of engaging in the informal economy. It was asserted that this can be achieved by increasing the penalties and probability of detection.

Table 3.3 The causes of unemployment (the results of the unemployed evaluation)

No.	Causal factors	Mean value	Mode	Min value	Max value
1.	One's qualification does not correspond to the supply of jobs	3.40	4	1	4
2.	***Insufficiently high wages in the positions offered***	***3.67***	***4***	***1***	***4***
3.	The current social support system does not encourage people to look for a job	2.91	3	1	4
4.	***I live in a region with a high unemployment rate and cannot travel to larger cities due to high costs***	***3.69***	***4***	***1***	***4***
5.	The market no longer needs people of respectable age	2.56	2	1	4
6.	The market no longer needs workers with the degrees 2–3 of disability	2.41	2	1	4

Source: compiled by the authors based on own calculations

Table 3.4 The consequences of unemployment (the results of the expert evaluation)

No.	Consequential factors	Mean value	Mode	Min value	Max value
1.	Low risks of being caught in one's municipality	2.83	3	1	4
2.	Lack of trust in the authorities	2.79	3	1	4
3.	Insufficiently strong educational system affected by the negative impact of the informal labor market on the state	2.99	3	1	4
4.	***High official long-term unemployment rate, when income is earned in the informal labor market and is not declared***	***3.41***	***3***	***2***	***4***

Source: compiled by the authors based on own calculations

Examining how the expected penalties and probability of detection in Lithuania, the finding is that 13% of the respondents expect that imprisonment will occur in the case of income concealment. Most of the respondents (61%) believe that in such cases it will be expected that the payment of the tax and social contributions due will be expected and in addition there will be a fine. A further 25% expect that payment the payment of the tax and social contributions due will be expected within a specified time and the remaining 2% state that they do not know.

Turning to the expected risk of detection in their municipality for people who work and do not declare their income, the finding is that 40% rate the risk very high, 40% rate the risk high, and just 15% rate the risk low and 5% very low. Examining how they expect to be detected, 48% believe that offences are mainly detected by responding to the population's complaints, 23% of the respondents are of the opinion that offences are detected during scheduled inspections, and 21% think that they are detected by chance.

In recent decades, it has been recognized that even when the expected benefits of participating in the informal economy outweigh the expected costs, many still do not participate. To explain this, a neo-institutional theoretical perspective has been adopted in which citizens are viewed as social actors rather than rational economic actors. This views participation in the informal economy as driven by the institutions. Institutions are the rules of the game in a society. According to a variant of institutional theory applied to explain participation in the informal economy, every society has both formal institutions describing the laws and regulations, as well as informal institutions describing the norms, beliefs, and values of citizens and consumers about the acceptability of different behaviors (Helmke & Levitsky, 2004; North, 1990). Using this institutionalist lens, the informal economy is seen to fall outside the regulations of formal institutions but within the acceptable behavior defined by the norms, values and beliefs of the informal institutions (Williams, 2017). Therefore, participation in informal economy appears when there is an asymmetry between the two types of institution. When the informal institutions, namely citizens, employers, and workers view participation in the informal economy as socially legitimate endeavor, there is greater participation in the informal economy. This institutional asymmetry arises when there is a lack of trust in what authorities are seeking to achieve (for a review, see Williams & Horodnic, 2020).

In this study, this theoretical explanation has been analyzed. As shown above, different forms of informal economic activity are widely viewed as socially legitimate and acceptable forms of economic activity. To repeat, 43% of the respondents find acceptable income non-declaring when an individual person or a self-employed evades taxes by hiding all or a part of one's income; 41% of the respondents find acceptable income non-declaring when a firm hires an individual person and pays a part of the wages informally ("envelope wages"); 38% find it acceptable when a firm hires another firm and business activities are not declared to the authorities; 36% find it acceptable when a business is hired by a private household and the income is not declared to the tax and social security authorities; and 29% find it acceptable when a private person is hired by another household and the income is not declared to the authorities. This reinforces the view that the informal institutions in Lithuania are not in symmetry with the formal institutions.

One of the major determinants of this institutional asymmetry is the lack of trust in public authorities (Williams, 2017). To evaluate the level of trust in public authorities in Lithuanian, the respondents were asked about their level of trust in different state institutions. The finding is that the unemployed in Lithuania trust the State Social Insurance Fund Board under the Ministry of Social Security and Labor (mean value is equal to 3.39), followed by the Migration Department under the Ministry of the Interior of the Republic of Lithuania (mean value is equal to 3.31) and the Employment Service under the Ministry of Social Security and Labor of the Republic of Lithuania (mean value is equal to 3.26). The highest distrust was expressed in relation to the State Tax Inspectorate (with the lowest mean value of 2.96) (see Fig. 3.4). The evaluations indicate that there are no unemployed who completely trust public authorities.

Meanwhile, according to the experts, this institutional perspective is accepted. For them, the lack of trust is one of the main reasons that makes society tolerate the existence of the informal labor market. Before turning towards the resultant policy solutions, attention first turns towards examining the relationship between the unemployment rate the informal economy across municipalities.

3.2.3 *The Relationship Between the Unemployment Rate and the Informal Economy in Municipalities*

The issues of long-term unemployment in Lithuanian municipalities with regard to agents' participation in the informal economy, especially over the period of the COVID-19 pandemic, have not been researched thus far. Evaluating the relationship

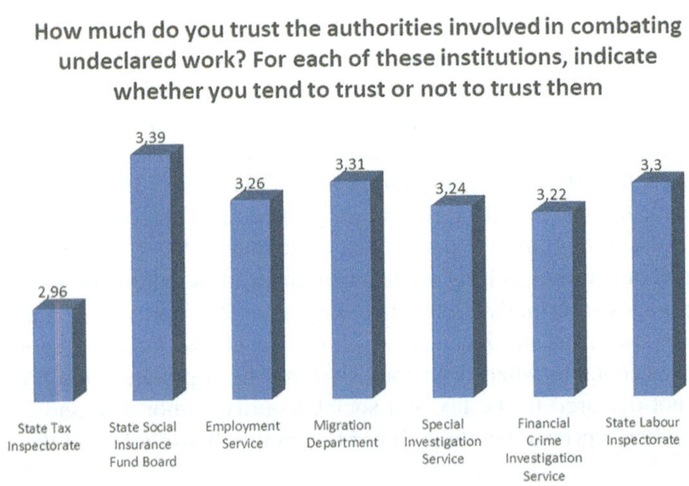

Fig. 3.4 Trust in public authorities, mean values

between the unemployment rate and the size of the informal economy discloses that 93% of Lithuanian municipalities have the negative relationship, except for those that have a very weak relationship. In terms of linearity, the values of the Pearson correlation coefficient showed the strongest correlation between the variables in Visaginas and Marijampolė municipalities. The results revealed that when the unemployment rate is fluctuating, the size of the informal economy is moving in the opposite direction. These findings can be explained by the fact that a significant proportion of workers operating in the informal economy are not included in the official labor force statistics due to the hidden nature of their informal activities. Thus, the officially announced employment statistics do not reflect the real employment rate in the labor market, which, in its turn, leads to an overestimated unemployment rate.

The correlations allow understanding of the real relationship between the unemployment rate and the size of the informal economy in Lithuanian municipalities, especially in those where the above-mentioned relationship is very strong. The strongest relationship between the size of the informal economy and the unemployment rate was found in Visaginas and Marijampolė municipalities, while only the median showed that the unemployment rate in Visaginas amounted to 11.8%, and in Marijampolė – to 11.2%. Both of these municipalities are among the ones with the highest unemployment rates, following Lazdijai (15%), Ignalina (14.9%), Kalvarija (14.6%), Akmenė (14.5%), Jurbarkas (14%), and Zarasai (14%) municipalities. The causes explaining the relationship identified during the empirical research are as follows: (1) the Lithuanian system of granting social benefits in terms of their amount and provision promotes unemployment, which, in its turn, leads to the spread of the informal economy when economic agents start operating in the informal labor market and at the same time receive social benefits; (2) regional exclusion in particular municipalities has contributed to the large number of the unemployed that has been growing throughout the period since restoration of the country's independence, which has resulted in the favorable conditions for the informality to thrive in the forms such as "envelope wages," dependent self-employment with undeclared or partially declared income, and work in the areas of housecleaning, beauty treatments, construction, agriculture, childcare, and repair services without concluding any formal employment contracts.

Annex 4 presents the correlation coefficients that reflect the relationship between the informal economy (as a % of GDP) and the unemployment rate in each municipality over the 2001–2019 period. The correlation coefficients reflect whether it is a very weak, weak, moderate, strong, and very strong relationship between the variables. 48% of the municipalities have a moderate correlation and 32% a strong correlation. Nevertheless, the correlation is negative in 93% of the municipalities, except only those where the correlation was found to be very weak. Although the Pearson and MCD correlation coefficients were found to be similar in most municipalities, the situation in Molėtai and Elektrėnai is different. The Pearson correlation coefficient estimated for Molėtai indicated that there is no significant relationship between the variables (0.01) in this municipality, although the MCD correlation coefficient indicates a moderate negative (−0.43) relationship. Similarly, the

Pearson correlation coefficient estimated for Elektrėnai is weak (−0.14), although the MCD correlation coefficient indicates a moderate negative (−0.43) relationship. To explain the negative relationship between the variables in Lithuania, Okun's law can be employed: an increasing/decreasing unemployment rate leads to a decrease/ an increase in the size of the informal economy.

In sum, 93% of Lithuanian municipalities have a negative relationship between the unemployment rate and the size of the informal economy. For a deeper analysis of the relationship between the unemployment rate and the informal economy, the results of the expert evaluation can be examined. The causes provided by the experts to explain this phenomenon are fivefold.

Firstly, for a number of years, Lithuania has had a flawed system of social benefits, which leads to deep-rooted long-term unemployment and creates preconditions for the informal economy to prosper. The COVID-19 pandemic has only exacerbated this problem. The long-term unemployment rate – one of the main indicators of exclusion – has jumped upwards (as of June 2021, the number of the long-term unemployed reached 41.9%). The growing curve of the number of the long-term unemployed indicates that long-term unemployment is a complex phenomenon, and the COVID-19 crisis is only one of the determinants. The COVID-19 pandemic has severely hampered application of the social inclusion and active inclusion measures (i.e., active labor market policies) and has further pushed the unemployed out of the formal labor market. The population that has been dropped out of the formal labor market and receives only very little monetary support (about 20–25% of the at-risk-of-poverty threshold) is thus marginalized, which means that a substantial part of this population are forced to work in the informal labor market or buy goods and services in informal markets. Social benefits are not subject to taxation, which makes them attractive as long-term income, and when the benefit period expires, the status of an unemployed person is abolished and a person is likely to start operating informally (i.e., a decreasing number of the official unemployed leads to an increasing number of informal labor market participants).

Secondly, the wages for unskilled jobs and social benefits are similar, which makes formal work and tax paying unattractive (wages are subject to taxation, while social benefits are not).

Thirdly, employers have no interest in paying higher formal wages. In addition, the persons with bailiffs' claims for debt repayment are not motivated to enter into formal employment contracts, which determines the negative relationship between the officially registered unemployment rate and the informal economy because informally employed persons remain registered as the unemployed. As a result, the official unemployment rate remains high and the informal labor market is thriving.

Fourthly, an increasing/decreasing unemployment rate leads to a decrease/ increase in the size of the informal economy. One of the causes of this relationship is that during the years of Lithuania's independence, the number of jobs in regions has dramatically decreased, which has promoted participation in the informal economy. The number of jobs in small towns and villages is shrinking further. Thus, the locals prioritize living on benefits and other undeclared income and tolerate the informal economy.

Fifth and finally, the unemployment rate in an individual municipality is significantly affected by the forms and amounts of the social benefits available. The unemployment rate can statistically significantly affect the size of the informal economy only in large municipalities because small ones detect only petty offences. The phenomenon of impunity is flourishing since effective control of small municipalities is too costly for the authorities.

Chapter 4
Conclusions and Recommendations

This final chapter provides a summary of firstly, the in-depth literature review of the informal economy and the relationship between unemployment and the informal economy. Secondly, it reports the findings of the survey conducted in Lithuania regarding the participation of the unemployed in the informal economy, and third and finally, it attempts to draw out some policy implications.

The review of the literature on the informal economy revealed that the most common definitions of the informal economy can be categorized as fiscal, market (economic), legal, and statistical. Reviewing the profile of an economic agent operating in the informal labor market, the various economic, demographic, and personal (ego) characteristics that reflect an agent's socio-economic status, personality, and environment were reviewed. Economic factors were shown to be the major determinants of an agent's participation in the informal labor market, although it is recognized that the decision to operate informally can also be affected by an agent's demographic characteristics (education, place of residence, gender, age, marital status, social status, and ethnicity) as well as their personal and behavioral characteristics. It was also recognized that there exists an upper-tier of agency-oriented informal workers who operate in the informal economy out of choice and a lower-tier of necessity-driven informal workers who operate in the informal economy as a survival tactic in the absence of alternative means of livelihood. The workers in these upper and lower tiers also often engage in different types of informal work, with those in the upper tier more likely to be engaged in own-account work in a self-employed basis and those in the lower tier more likely to be engaged in informal wage employment. Nevertheless, there are multifarious forms of informality and the literature review distinguished forms of informality by the employment status, whether engagement is by necessity or choice (i.e., motive), the degree of (non) formalization, the form of settlement (payment), and the activity premises (activity space).

Turning to the determinants of the informal economy, both at the rural and urban levels, the literature was shown to reveal that informality is strongly affected by

L. Gasparėnienė et al., *Unemployment and the Informal Economy*, SpringerBriefs in Economics, https://doi.org/10.1007/978-3-030-96687-4_4

general economic determinants but also the complexity of formal business regulation. From a market perspective, informality is determined by cost reduction and fierce market competition pressures. There are also public sector determinants of informality, with the major ones being corruption, weak rule of law and a lack of accountability, and low quality of public services (in terms of infrastructure, social protection, etc.). Meanwhile, the impact of social determinants on informality manifests itself through social values, the level of awareness of the costs of informality and benefits of formality, the relationship between personal and common (state) property and the relative interpretation of cultural, social, and legal norms. Finally, there are financial market determinants manifested through the availability of financing (loans, credits).

The literature also revealed that informal employment is not always associated with either a better or worse quality of life compared with formal employment. Although informal employment can provide relatively good economic benefits, social connections and the feeling of satisfaction, informally operating economic agents often face the problems of occupational safety and health (both physical and mental), they may have limited access to knowledge and in most cases lack social security coverage. In other words, it revealed the need for a more nuanced and finer-grained understanding of the impacts of participation in the informal economy on quality of life.

Finally, and reviewing the existent literature on the relationship between the informal economy and unemployment, it revealed that although the vast majority of previous studies confirm the existence of a positive relationship between unemployment rate and the informal economy and that only a small number of studies provide empirical evidence that this relationship can be negative or neutral, it is not always clear whether the relationship is temporary or permanent in nature. Indeed, it revealed that the strength and direction of the relationship between the unemployment rate and the informal economy can be determined by the target period (short or long run, a phase of an economic cycle – a period of an economic upswing or recession), the method selected for measuring unemployment rate and/or the size of the informal economy, the lag factor, and other determinants. In addition, the direction and intensity of this relationship may significantly vary in the context of developed and developing economies. All of this indicated that although there is quite a lot of studies focused on the issue under consideration, the general understanding of the interdependence between the unemployment rate and the informal economy is still limited. It is for this reason that the rest of this book then reported a study that examines this issue in Lithuania.

The survey of over 1000 unemployed people conducted in Lithuania during late 2020 revealed that that 92% of the unemployed know about one or more persons working informally. This displays the embeddedness of informality as a perceived social norm. Turning to whether they had engaged in informal work, 68% of the unemployed respondents have received unofficial income. The remaining 32% has not operated in the informal labor market while unemployed. This reveals, therefore, the prevalence of participation in the informal economy amongst the unemployed in Lithuania. Examining the type of informal work in which they engaged, most had engaged in housekeeping, construction, and/or agricultural work. That is, 40% of those participating in the informal economy had engaged in housecleaning, 21% in construction work, 23% worked in the agricultural sector, and 8% provided repair services, 4% provided beauty services, and 4% childcare services.

Indeed, examining whether they view engaging in informal work as acceptable, the finding was that 62% of all respondents indicate that they view participation in informal economic activities as acceptable, providing further support for the view that informality is perceived as a socially legitimate activity in Lithuania. Breaking this down to see if some types of informal work are viewed as more acceptable to engage in than others, the finding is that this is not necessarily the case. That is, 43% of the respondents find acceptable income non-declaring when an individual person or a self-employed evades taxes by hiding all or a part of one's income; 41% of the respondents find acceptable income non-declaring when a firm hires an individual person and pays a part of the wages informally ("envelope wages"); 38% find it acceptable when a firm hires another firm and business activities are not declared to the authorities; 36% find it acceptable when a business is hired by a private household and the income is not declared to the tax and social security authorities; and 29% find it acceptable when a private person is hired by another household and the income is not declared to the authorities.

Moreover, 75% of the respondents see no reason why they should not accept undeclared income from an employer. Of all respondents, 49% would any amount and 26% only small amounts. Just 25% would not accept such undeclared income from an employer. Turning to whether this has occurred in practice when they had been working, 30% of all respondents had accepted undeclared income from an employer, and only 17% had refused such income. The remaining 53% stated that they did not know.

As such, this survey reveals that over two-thirds (68%) of the unemployed respondents had worked in the informal economy while they were unemployed.

How, therefore, can this participation in the informal economy be tackled? As Chap. 3 revealed, there is a need to address not only the cost-benefit ratio confronting potential participants in the informal economy but also the perceived acceptability of participation in the informal economy, manifested in the widespread perception that this is a socially legitimate economic activity in which to engage. In the following, we report initiatives recommended by the expert groups to achieve these objectives.

To tackle the informal economy, the State Labor Inspectorate could not only improve the perceived and actual risk of detection and review the system of fines but could also engage in awareness raising campaigns to highlight the benefits of formality and costs of informality. Given the results of the research, inspections could focus upon agricultural, construction, and repair service, perhaps using announced inspections so that the unemployed know that these sectors in which they predominantly work are being targeted. It also requires education and awareness raising to be conducted by the labor inspectorate among the unemployed who perceive informal work as a socially legitimate activity. This could focus upon explaining the benefits of paying tax and social insurance contributions such as in relation to the provision of better health care services.

Regarding actions that can be taken by the state tax inspectorate, the intention again must be to increase the perceived and actual likelihood of detection and penalties, but also to educate and raise awareness about the benefits of formality and costs of informality. Examples of the policy initiatives that could be undertaken include the following:

- Creating a network of municipal social partners involving not only representatives of state institutions (the Employment Service, elderships, Labor Inspectorate, police, etc.), but also civic organizations (communities, elders' meetings, etc.) to improve information sharing and to better understand the specifics of the labor market in each municipality.
- To unify the conditions of business operation (i.e., to ensure that a certain type of activity such as rural tourism is carried out based on the same form of license (e.g., an individual activity certificate, a farmer's license). Currently, the variety of business organization forms is very wide (e.g., rural tourism activities can be carried out based on either an individual activity certificate or a farmer's license), which creates preconditions for not declaring income and evading taxes. Simplification of registration, therefore, is required.
- To introduce the requirement of a universal declaration of income and assets.
- To digitize accounting systems that would prevent informal activities in municipalities, especially in the areas of construction, repair (cars, housing), childcare, health care services, housecleaning, relocation, passenger transporting, hairdressing, and beauty treatments.
- In co-operation with bailiffs' offices, register/monitor indebted residents who, due to their indebtedness, evade working in the official market or only partially declare their official work income. Employers also tend to take advantage of this situation and pay only minimum wages.
- To increase the frequency of inspections of the following economic activities: construction, repair, childcare, health care services, housecleaning, relocation, passenger transporting, hairdressing, and beauty treatments, which are the main sectors in which informality takes place.
- To abolish the receipts issued for agricultural and forestry services or tighten up the procedure for issuing the receipts because currently the receipts are often abused to disguise the employment relationship, which leads to the spread of informal activities.
- To reduce the circulation of cash by introducing a mandatory transfer of wages to digital accounts in the areas of construction, beauty treatments, and other economic activities characterized by the highest implicit rates of undeclared work.
- To organize more frequent inspection campaigns, such as requesting a receipt at the markets.
- To attract a larger number of qualified specialists to the Control Department and to address the problem of low remuneration coefficients for the specialists who conduct inspections.

Meanwhile, the Ministry of Social Security and Labor of the Republic of Lithuania could:

- Strengthen co-operation between the Employment Service and municipalities to ascertain whether a person registered with the Employment Service has also applied to the municipality for social benefits. This will help to identify the persons who apply to the Employment Service only to be granted the compulsory health insurance.
- Strengthen inter-institutional co-operation among the State Labor Inspectorate, the Employment Service, and the State Tax Inspectorate to establish the principles for the exchange of the data on the activities of the labor force at risk.
- Review the functions of the Employment Service so that this institution is responsible for providing the real help for jobseekers and organizing professional development/vocational training/courses rather than providing social benefits.
- Carry out more in-depth systematic studies to identify the personal causes of long-term unemployment and to organize more intensive work of social workers with persons at social risk and the ones with the status of a long-term unemployed.
- Raise the wages for unskilled work in regions and to reduce the amounts of social benefits, i.e. to widen the gap between the amount of wages and the amount of social benefits.
- Reduce perhaps workplace taxes, especially in regions with the highest unemployment rates; to reduce taxes for employers and promote subsidy payments in the cases of concluding long-term employment contracts, which could help prevent "envelope wages"; to reduce taxes for the self-employed who operate in the market under a business license or an individual activity certificate (in many cases, they operate together with other persons whose activities are not formalized).
- Reduce the duration of one's unemployment status with the Employment Service.
- Reduce the amount of social benefits paid to the long-term unemployed.
- Intensify the control of job search in the Employment Service; to raise the attractiveness of the Employment Service to employers because currently they tend to announce only unattractive vacancies; to reduce the requirements for the unemployed to participate in the active labor market programs, taking into account the needs of a particular municipality.
- Organize training for the long-term unemployed to help them establish themselves in the labor market; after one refuses some job offers, to abolish one's status of the unemployed with the Employment Service, stop payment of benefits and compensations for utilities.
- In the case a person starts business operation under an individual activity certificate or a business license, to allow payment of only the compulsory health insurance contributions and exempt this person from paying other taxes for at least the first year from the commencement of the new activity.
- Review the benefit granting procedures and benefit amounts; the benefits should not be paid to young, healthy, able-bodied persons; those who receive social

benefits should be required to perform community services; the amounts of benefits should be differentiated based on the number of hours spent on the community service, i.e. the more hours a person works, the higher benefit he/she receives; the ceiling of the benefit would generate the need to find a paid job.
- Decouple granting the compulsory health insurance from one's registration with the Employment Service because currently many persons register with the Employment Service only to evade paying the compulsory health insurance contributions.
- Address workers' transport problems by organizing their transporting to workplaces or by reimbursing the costs of commuting to work.
- Profile the unemployed to identify the ones who are not ready for the labor market, and thus raise the potential for more effective application of the employment promotion measures targeted at the unemployed who are willing to return to the labor market.

Many of these measures will deal with the problem of informality once it has occurred. To prevent participation in the informal economy from occurring, however, there is a need to address the trust in public institutions. Public trust in institutional authorities tends to decline sharply due to corruption, poor and/or invisible performance of public institutions, and the low quality of governance (World Bank, 2017). It also tends to decline with the growing expectations of citizens (when the public sector fails, is unwilling or unable to respond to the growing needs of the citizens) and is closely related to the condition of the national economy (public confidence in institutional authorities is usually higher in developed economies).

To address this issue, Kettl (2017) distinguishes between "wholesale" and "retail" dimensions of increasing public confidence in institutional authorities. At the wholesale (macro) level, the main measure is involving citizens in decision-making, while at the retail (micro) level public confidence can be promoted by improving citizens' experience of daily interaction with public authorities. To implement the above-mentioned dimensions, the following practical solutions are provided:

- involvement of representatives of the public in budget allocation and public expenditure planning (especially at the municipal level) - this measure is proposed as a way to better align budgetary and public spending decisions with citizens' priorities and values;
- a clear division of responsibilities among public servants (citizens must have easy access to the information on which public servant in a particular institution is in charge of the problems in question, which area this servant is responsible for and what consultations he/she provides) - this measure is proposed to increase transparency of institutional work, to separate servants' functions, and to ensure accountability (the Finnish example);
- promotion of the use of e-government and online social platforms for daily interaction between citizens and public authorities - this measure is proposed to ensure citizens' participation in the delivery of public services, to identify the relevant problems, and to find solutions to these problems;

- reporting to citizens on where and how tax money is being used and was used in the previous period – this measure is proposed to promote public confidence in the national tax system, which, in its turn, contributes to public confidence in institutional authorities;
- dissemination of the information about positive achievements and positive practices (solving specific problems of the citizens, implementation of particular projects, benefits of the projects to community members, co-operation between public institutions and communities) through mass media – this measure is proposed as a way to increase public confidence that municipal budget funds are not wasted for unnecessary projects (the US example);
- development of free legal aid for citizens – this measure is proposed as a way to help citizens defend their rights, reduce confusion and misunderstandings arising from ever-changing laws, and differing interpretations of laws;
- regular surveys of citizens' trust in public authorities – this measure is proposed as a way to monitor the dynamics of citizens' trust/distrust in public authorities, identify the existing problems, and assess the progress (the Finnish example).

In sum, this book has been one of the first to evaluate the relationship between unemployment and the informal economy and what might be done to tackle this phenomenon. It reveals that there is a paucity of research on this relationship and the need for further research in other countries and global regions. If this book stimulates such research, then it will have achieved one of its intentions. However, this book also reveals the need for action to be taken to prevent participation in the informal economy by the unemployed. This book has begun to highlight the wide range of policy initiatives required to tackle this phenomenon. These range from policy initiatives to increase the perceived and actual costs of participating in the informal economy through policy initiatives to increase the actual or perceived benefits of formality to policy measures to improve trust in public institutions, ranging from modernization of public institutions to education and awareness raising campaigns on the benefits of formality and costs of informality. It also shows the wider range of institutions that need to be involved in tackling this phenomenon. Indeed, specific policy initiatives that could be undertaken in Lithuania by a range of institutions have been proposed. If public authorities in other countries begin to consider and develop such a wider range of policy measures for tackling the informal economy, then this book will have fulfilled its wider intention.

Annex 1: Youth Unemployment Rate in the EU Member States as of January 2021

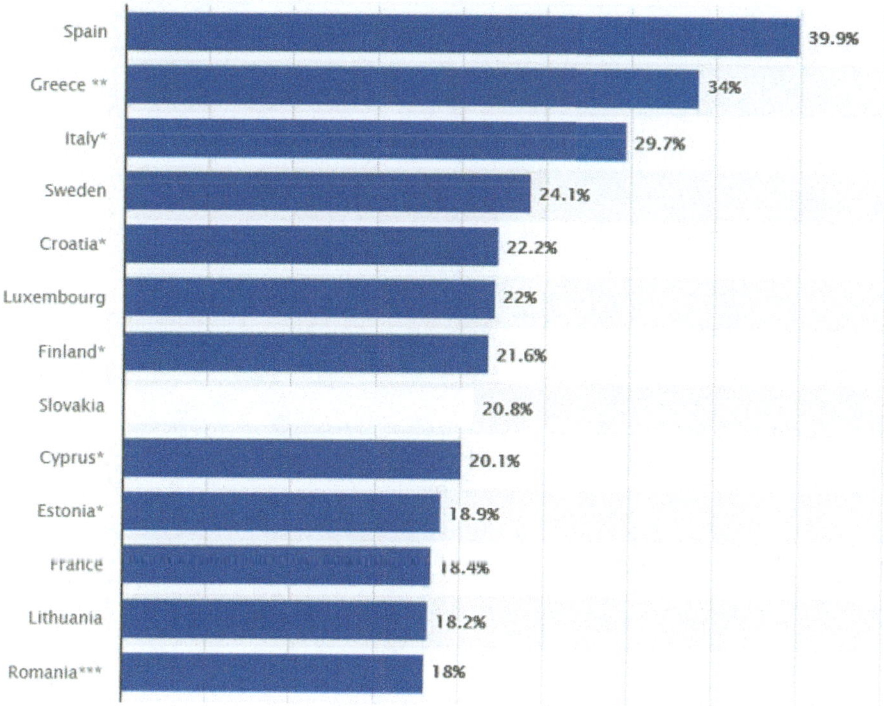

Source: https://www.statista.com/statistics/266228/youth-unemployment-rate-in-eu-countries/

L. Gasparėnienė et al., *Unemployment and the Informal Economy*, SpringerBriefs in Economics, https://doi.org/10.1007/978-3-030-96687-4

Annex 2: QUESTIONNAIRE

Part I. Demographic data:

1. **Your age:**
   - 18 – 25
   - 26 – 35
   - 36 – 45
   - 46 – 55
   - 56 – 65
   - 66 and older
2. **Gender:**
   - Female.
   - Male.
3. **How long have you been unemployed?**
   - Up to 3 months.
   - Up to half a year.
   - More than half a year.
   - A year and longer.
4. **Municipality where you reside:**
   Please, specify: ....
5. **Education:**
   - Higher.
   - Post-secondary.
   - Secondary.
   - Other.

L. Gasparėnienė et al., *Unemployment and the Informal Economy*, SpringerBriefs in Economics, https://doi.org/10.1007/978-3-030-96687-4

6. **Citizenship:**

- Lithuanian.
- Russian.
- Polish.
- Other (please, specify).......

Part II. Identification of the causal and consequential factors that affect involvement of the unemployed in the (labor) informality

7. **Do you personally know any people who work without declaring all or a part of their income to social security institutions? (please, select one answer).**

- Yes, I know one or two persons.
- Yes, I know some persons (more than two).
- No.

8. **In your opinion, what sanction can be imposed for concealing income?**

- Payment of the regular tax or social insurance contribution due, i.e. debt repayment before a specified time.
- Payment of the regular tax or social insurance contribution due and a fine, i.e. debt repayment and fine payment before a specified time.
- Imprisonment.
- Other.

9. **People who work and do not declare their income run the risk of being fined. How would you describe the risk of being detected in your municipality?**

- Very high.
- Sufficiently high.
- Sufficiently low.
- Very low.

10. **In your opinion, in which ways do the authorities responsible for detecting the cases of not declaring income detect the offenses (envelope wages, evasion of social insurance contributions, and other taxes)?**

- At random.
- Respond to population's complaints.
- During scheduled inspections.
- Through the methodologies established in particular organizations.
- Other.

11. **Do you know any people in your environment who consume/trade smuggled goods (fuels, cigarettes, alcohol)?**

- Yes.
- No.

12. **Do you justify the use of smuggled goods/participation in smuggling activities?**

- Yes.
- No.

13. **What are the causes of your unemployment?**

	1 (I completely disagree)	2 (I disagree)	3 (I agree)	4 (I completely agree)
My qualification does not correspond to the supply of jobs				
Insufficiently high wages in the positions offered				
The current social support system does not encourage people to look for a job				
I live in a region with a high unemployment rate and cannot travel to larger cities due to high costs				
The market no longer needs people of respectable age				
The market no longer needs workers with the degrees 2–3 of disability				
Other ________________				

14. **How much do you trust the authorities involved in combating undeclared work? For each of these institutions, indicate whether you tend to trust or not to trust them (please, tick).**

	I completely do not trust (1)	I do not trust (2)	I trust (3)	I completely trust (4)
State Tax Inspectorate				
State Social Insurance Fund Board				
Employment Service				
Migration Department				
Special Investigation Service				
Financial Crime Investigation Service				
State Labor Inspectorate				

15. **How do you rate different following behaviors, to which extent you find particular behavior acceptable or unacceptable? (from "1" – completely unacceptable to "4" – completely acceptable).**

Question No.	Statement	1 (completely unacceptable)	2 (unacceptable)	3 (acceptable)	4 (completely acceptable)
1.	A firm hires an individual person and pays a part of the wages informally				
2.	A firm is hired by another company and business activities are not declared to tax or social security institutions				
3.	A private person is hired by a household and the income is not declared to tax or social security institutions, although it has to be declared				
4.	A firm is hired by a private household for particular works and the income is not declared to tax or social security institutions				
5.	An individual person or a self-employed evades taxes by hiding all or a part of one's income				

16. **Over the period of the last 12 months, have you paid for any good or services realizing that the income earned from these goods or services was not likely to be declared (e.g., no receipt or VAT invoice was issued)?**

- Yes.
- No.
- I do not know.

17. **For which of the following goods or services have your paid over the period of the last 12 months realizing that the transaction was based on undeclared work, i.e. the income was not likely to be declared to tax or social security institutions?**

- Childcare.
- Health care services.
- Hairdressing or beauty treatments.
- Cleaning or ironing.
- Home repair and improvement.
- Gardening.
- Teaching.
- Relocation.
- Passenger transporting.
- Assistance for a dependent of an elderly person.
- Administrative or clerical tasks, or IT assistance.
- Repair services (e.g., mobile phones, cars, etc.)
- Purchase of food (e.g., farm products).
- Purchase of other goods or services.
- I have not paid for such goods or services (please, skip question 18).

18. **Why did you buy these goods or services in the informal rather than formal market?**

- Lower price.
- Faster service.
- Better quality.
- With the intention to help a person who needs money.
- It was a favor to friends, relatives or colleagues.
- The good or service can hardly be found in the formal market.
- I only later realized that it was not going to be declared.
- Other.

19. **Would you accept income from your employer knowing that the income is going to be declared to tax institutions?**

- Yes, any amount.
- Yes, small amounts.
- No.

20. **When you were working, did you ever refuse income from your employer because you knew that the income is undeclared?**

- Yes.
- No.
- I do not know.

21. **Over the period of your official unemployment, have you ever earned or searched for external income from short-term orders that were paid for in cash/unofficially?**

- Yes (if your answer is "yes," go to question 22).
- No (go to question 23).

22. **What orders did you complete?**

- Worked in agriculture.
- Provided childcare services.
- Provided housecleaning services.
- Did construction works.
- Provided beauty services.
- Provided repair services.
- Other (please, specify).

23. **What measures would you recommend for reducing long-term unemployment in your municipality more effectively?**

- Tax relief for newly established businesses for the first 1–2 years of operating.
- Raising average wages.
- Reduction of social benefits, taking into account a person's health condition.
- Other.

Annex 3

Dear Expert,

I. GENERAL INFORMATION ABOUT AN EXPERT:

1. Which municipality do you represent?
(List of municipalities)
2. Your position:
Mayor.
Employment Service.
Ministry of Social Security and Labor of the Republic of Lithuania.
State Tax Inspectorate under the Ministry of Finance of the Republic of Lithuania

II. CAUSAL AND CONSEQUENTIAL FACTORS AFFECTING INVOLVEMENT OF THE UNEMPLOYED IN INFORMALITY.

1. Based on the Likert scale, please, evaluate which **causal factors** have the greatest impact on involvement of the unemployed in the informal labor market? (from 1 – *I completely disagree with the statement* to 4 – *I completely agree with the statement*).

No.	Causal factors	1 (I completely disagree)	2 (I disagree)	3 (I agree)	4 (I completely agree)
1.	Living on the benefit, an unemployed selects cheaper smuggled goods				
2.	Wages in regions are insufficiently high; as a result, the amount of social benefits demotivates the unemployed to search for a paid job				
3.	Justification of informal activities when purchasing undeclared goods/services				

L. Gasparėnienė et al., *Unemployment and the Informal Economy*, SpringerBriefs in Economics, https://doi.org/10.1007/978-3-030-96687-4

No.	Causal factors	1 (I completely disagree)	2 (I disagree)	3 (I agree)	4 (I completely agree)
4.	The potential not to declare income and at the same time receive unemployment benefits				
5.	Prolonged operation without declaring one's income caused by long-term unemployment				
6.	Lack of public awareness				
7.	Other (please, specify)				

2. Based on the Likert scale, please, evaluate which **consequential factors** have the greatest impact on involvement of the unemployed in the informal labor market? (from 1 – *I completely disagree with the statement* to 5 – *I completely agree with the statement*).

No.	Consequential factors	1 (I completely disagree)	2 (I disagree)	3 (I agree)	4 (I completely agree)
1.	Low risks of being caught in one's municipality				
2.	Lack of trust in the authorities				
3.	Insufficiently strong educational system affected by the negative impact of the informal labor market on the state				
4.	High official long-term unemployment rate, when income is earned in the informal labor market and is not declared				
5.	Other (please, specify)				

3. The correlation analysis between the unemployment rate and the shadow economy (% of GDP) in Lithuanian municipalities revealed that 48 percent of municipalities have a moderate, and 32 percent – a strong correlation between the variables. Nevertheless, the correlation between the unemployment rate and the size of the shadow economy is negative in 93 percent of the municipalities, except only those where the correlation was found to be very weak. The results revealed that when the unemployment rate is fluctuating, the size of the shadow economy is moving in the opposite direction. The negative relationship means that a decreasing/an increasing unemployment rate leads to an increasing/a decreasing size of the shadow economy. How would you explain this phenomenon in your municipality? (an open-ended question).
4. The group of the researchers are of the opinion that the main cause of this relationship is that a significant proportion of workers operating in the informal economy are not included in the official labor force statistics due to the

hidden nature of their informal activities. Thus, the officially announced employment statistics do not reflect the real employment rate in the labor market, which, in its turn, leads to an overestimated unemployment rate.

- I agree.
- I disagree (if you marked this answer, please, provide the arguments why).

5. Please, provide the recommendations on how both the size of the shadow economy and the unemployment rate could be reduced in **your municipality** (an open-ended question).

Recommendation to the State Tax Inspectorate: how to extract undeclared/hidden income from the shadows?

Recommendation to the Ministry of Social Security and Labor of the Republic of Lithuania: how to promote employment and increase motivation of the unemployed in individual municipalities?

Recommendation to the State Labor Inspectorate.

References

Abada, F. C., Manasseh, C. O., Nwakoby, I., Iroegbu, N. F., Okoh, J. I., Alio, F., Lawal, A. I., & Asogwa, O. J. (2021). Relationship between unemployment rate and shadow economy in Nigeria: A Tado-Yamamoto approach. *International Journal of Financial Research, 12*(3), 271–283. https://doi.org/10.5430/ijfr.v12n3p271

Abdih, Y., & Medina, L. (2013). *Measuring the informal economy in the Caucasus and Central Asia*. IMF Working paper No. 13/137. Retrieved from https://www.imf.org/en/Publications/WP/Issues/2016/12/31/Measuring-the-Informal-Economy-in-the-Caucasus-and-Central-Asia-40621.

Abdlaziz, R. A., Ali, F., & Abdulkadhim, H. (2020). Relationship between unemployment rate and shadow economy of selected mena countries a toda-yamamoto and panel causality approach. *Qalaai Zanist Scientific Journal, 5*(4), 896–916. https://doi.org/10.25212/lfu.qzj.5.4.32

Abraham, R. (2017). *Informal workers in formal and informal enterprises in India: A comparative analysis*. Retrieved June 23, 2021, from http://conference.iza.org/conference_files/Statistic_2017/abraham_r25068.pdf.

Adom, K. (2014). Beyond the marginalization thesis: An examination of the motivations of informal entrepreneurs in sub-Saharan Africa: Insights from Ghana. *International Journal of Entrepreneurship and Innovation, 15*(2), 113–125.

Agarwala, R. (2013). *Informal labor, formal politics, and dignified discontent in India*. Cambridge University Press.

Alanon, A., & Gomez-Antonio, M. (2005). Estimating the size of the shadow economy in Spain: A structural model with latent variable. *Applied Economics, 37*, 1011–1025.

Alexandru Davidescu (2013). *The relationship between shadow economy and unemployment rate. A ARDL causality analysis for the case of Romania*. Retrieved June 28, 2021, from https://ec.europa.eu/eurostat/cros/system/files/NTTS2013fullPaper_239.pdf.

Alexandru, A. A., Dobre, I., & Ghinararu, C. C. (2010). Revisiting the relationship between unemployment rate and the size of the shadow economy for United States using Johansen approach for cointegration. In *Proceedings of the 11th WSEAS international conference on mathematics and computers in business and economics and 11th WSEAS international conference on biology and chemistry* (pp. 199–204).

Allingham, M. G., & Sandmo, A. (1972). Income tax evasion: A theoretical analysis. *Journal of Public Economics, 1*(3–4), 323–338. https://doi.org/10.1016/0047-2727(72)90010-2

L. Gasparėnienė et al., *Unemployment and the Informal Economy*, SpringerBriefs in Economics, https://doi.org/10.1007/978-3-030-96687-4

Almenar, V., Sanchez, J. L., & Sapena, J. (2020). Measuring the shadow economy and its drivers: The case of peripheral EMU countries. *Economic Research – Ekonomska Istraživanja, 33*(1), 2904–2918. https://doi.org/10.1080/1331677X.2019.1706601

Altbeker, A., & Storme, E. (2013). *Graduate unemployment in South Africa: A much exaggerated problem*. Retrieved April 30, 2021, from https://cde.org.za/wp-content/uploads/2018/07/Graduate-unemployment-in-South-Africa-A-much-exaggerated-problem-CDE-Insight.pdf.

Alvarez, C. V., Potes, M. P. E., & Merchan, M. E. P. (2016). Quality of life and informal labor among elderly persons in an intermediate Colombian city, 2012–2013. *Revista Brasileira de Geriatria e Gerontologia, 19*(3), 415–427. https://doi.org/10.1590/1809-98232016019.140215

Amaral, P. S., & Quintin, E. (2006). A competitive model of the informal sector. *Journal of Monetary Economics, 53*(7), 1541–1553. https://doi.org/10.1016/j.jmoneco.2005.07.016

Amasiatu, C. V., & Shah, M. H. (2014). First party fraud: A review of the forms and motives of fraudulent consumer behaviours in e-tailing. *International Journal of Retail & Distribution Management, 42*(9), 805–817.

Andrews, D., Caldera Sánchez, A., & Johansson, A. (2011). *Towards a better understanding of the informal economy*. OECD Economics Department Working Papers, No. 873. OECD Publishing. https://doi.org/10.1787/5kgb1mf88x28-en

Arsic, M., Arandarenko, B., Radulovic, B., Randelovic, S., & Jankovic, I. (2015). Causes of the shadow economy. In G. Krstic & F. Schneider (Eds.), *Formalizing the shadow economy in Serbia. Contributions to economics* (pp. 21–46). https://doi.org/10.1007/978-3-319-13437-6_4

Arunatilake, N., & Jayawardena, P. (2010). Why people choose to participate in the informal sector in Sri Lanka. *Indial Journal of Labor Economics, 53*(2), 225–249.

Augustinaitis, A., Rudzkiene, V., Petrauskas, R. A., Dagyte, I., Martinaityte, E., Leichteris, E., Malinauskiene, E., Visnevska, V., & Zilioniene, I. (2009). *Lietuvos e.valdzios gaires: Ateities izvalgu tyrimas*. Mykolas Romeris University. Retrieved from http://ebooks.mruni.eu/product/lietuvos-evaldios-gairs-ateities-valg-tyrimas25169#sthash.SWyBMnuZ.dpuf

Avirgan, T., Gammage, S., & Bivens, J. (2005). *Good jobs, bad jobs, no jobs. Labor markets and informal work in Egypt, El Salvador, India, Russia, and South Africa*. Retrieved May 20, 2021, from https://www.epi.org/publication/books_good_jobs/.

Awasthi, R., & Engelschalk, M. (2018). *Taxation and the shadow economy: How the tax system can stimulate and enforce the formalization of business activities*. Policy Research Working Paper, No. 8391. Washington, DC: World Bank. Retrieved from https://openknowledge.worldbank.org/handle/10986/29603.

Badita, A., Mazilu, M., & Popescu, L. (2015). Challenges for human capital and sustainable development of rural areas. A case study on Craiova metropolitan area, Romania. *Carpathian Journal of Earth and Environmental Sciences, 10*(3), 101–112.

Bajada, C., & Schneider, F. (2009). Unemployment and the shadow economy in the OECD. *Revue Economique, 60*(5), 1033–1067. https://doi.org/10.3917/reco.605.1033

Balabanova, D., & McKee, M. (2002). Understanding informal payments for health care: The example of Bulgaria. *Health Policy, 62*, 243–273. https://doi.org/10.1016/s0168-8510(02)00035-0

Banerjee, A. V., Hanna, R., Kreindler, G. E., & Olken, B. A. (2017). Debunking the stereotype of the lazy welfare recipient: Evidence from cash transfer programs. *The World Bank Research Observer, 32*, 155–184.

Banks, N., Lombard, M., & Mitlin, D. (2020). Urban informality as a site of critical analysis. *The Journal of Development Studies, 56*(2), 223–238. https://doi.org/10.1080/00220388.2019.1577384

Barbour, A., & Llanes, M. (2013). *Supporting people to legitimise their informal businesses*. Retrieved June 16, 2021, from https://www.jrf.org.uk/report/supporting-people-legitimise-their-informal-businesses.

Barrett, C. B., Reardon, T., & Webb, P. (2001). Nonfarm income diversification and household livelihood strategies in rural Africa: Concepts, dynamics, and policy implications. *Food Policy, 26*, 315–331.

Benson, E., Best, S., del Pozo-Vergnes, E., Garside, B., Mohammed, E. Y., Panhuysen. S., Piras, G.; Vorley, B., Walnycki, A., & Wilson, E. (2014). *Informal and green? The forgotten voice in the transition to a green economy*. Retrieved March 28, 2021, from http://pubs.iied.org/pdfs/16566IIED.pdf.

Bertranou, F., Casanova, L., Jiménez, M., & Jiménez, M. (2014). *Informality and employment quality in Argentina: Country case study on labor market segmentation*. Conditions of Work and Employment Series No. 49. Retrieved July 5, 2021, from http://www.oit.org/wcmsp5/groups/public/%2D%2D-ed_protect/%2D%2D-protrav/%2D%2D-travail/documents/publication/wcms.313839.pdf.

Beyer, A., & Morgan, B. (2018). *Motivations for engaging in entrepreneurial activity in the informal sector in Sub Saharan Africa*. Retrieved May 19, 2021, from https://www.diva-portal.org/smash/get/diva2:1228777/FULLTEXT01.pdf.

Bhan, G., Surie, A., Horwood, C., Dobson, R., Alfers, L., Portela, A., & Rollins, N. (2020). Informal work and maternal and child health: A blind spot in public health and research. *Bulletin of the World Health Organisation, 98*, 219–221. https://doi.org/10.2471/BLT.19.231258

Biderman, C., Smolka, M., & Sant'Anna, A. (2008). *Urban housing informality: Does building and land use regulation matter?* Retrieved June 21, 2021, from https://www.lincolninst.edu/sites/default/files/pubfiles/1405_721_LLA080704.pdf.

Bihunirwa, M., Kinyua, H., Mugoya, M., Shariff, M., & Rwakakamba, M. (2012). *Innovating to compete: Smallholder farmers' agency and markets in East Africa*. Retrieved March 29, 2021, from http://pubs.iied.org/pdfs/16520IIED.pdf.

Blackburn, K., Bose, N., & Capasso, S. (2012). Tax evasion, the underground economy and financial development. *Journal of Economic Behavior & Organization, 83*(2), 243–253.

Bonnet, F., Carre, F., & Vanek, J. (2019a). *Informal employment quality of employment framework—Experimental indicator (4a.x2)*. Retrieved May 23, 2021, from https://unece.org/fileadmin/DAM/stats/documents/ece/ces/ge.12/2019/S6_ILO_WIEGO.pdf.

Bonnet, F., Vanek, J., & Chen, M. (2019b). *Women and men in the informal economy: A statistical brief*. Retrieved May 17, 2021, from https://www.ilo.org/wcmsp5/groups/public/%2D%2D-ed_protect/%2D%2D-protrav/%2D%2D-travail/documents/publication/wcms_711798.pdf.

Bordignon, M., & Zanardi, A. (1997). Tax Evasion in Italy. *Giornale degli Economisti e Annali di Economia, 56*, 169–210.

Bosch, M., & Campos-Vazquez, R. M. (2014). The trade-offs of welfare policies in labor markets with informal jobs: The case of the "Seguro Popular" program in Mexico. *American Economic Journal: Economic Policy, 6*, 71–99.

Breach, R., Martínez, A., Montenegro, V., & Mateos, F. (2006). *Medición de la Evasión Fiscal en México*. Centro De Economía Aplicada Y Políticas Públicas Del ITAM.

Brief Methodological Analyses. (2012). *The shadow economy: How to measure and model it?* Retrieved May 25, 2021, from www.minfin.bg/document/9795:4.

Brill, L. (2011). *Women's participation in the informal economy: What can we learn from Oxfam's work?* Oxfam.

Brown, D., McGranahan, G., & Dodman, D. (2014). *Urban informality and building a more inclusive, resilient and green economy*. Retrieved June 22, 2021, from https://pubs.iied.org/sites/default/files/pdfs/migrate/10722IIED.pdf.

Bureau, S., & Fendt, J. (2011). Entrepreneurship in the informal economy: Why it matters. *International Journal of Entrepreneurship and Innovation, 12*(2), 85–94. https://doi.org/10.5367/ijei.2011.0026

Burger, P., & Fourie, F. (2019). The unemployed and the formal and informal sectors in South Africa: A macroeconomic analysis. *South African Journal of Economic and Management Sciences, 22*(1), 1–12. https://doi.org/10.4102/sajems.v22i1.2104

Černiauskas, G., & Dobravolskas, A. (2011). Emerging of market economy in Lithuania (1990–2010). *Intellectual Economics, 5*(3), 371–387.

CGAP. (2020). *Relief for informal workers: Falling through the cracks in COVID-19*. Retrieved July 02, 2021, from https://www.cgap.org/research/covid-19-briefing/relief-informal-workers-falling-through-cracks-covid-19.

Chambwera, M., Macgregor, J., & Baker, A. (2012). *Informal economy: Primer for development professionals on the importance of the informal economy in developing countries*. International Institute for Environment and Development. Retrieved from https://pubs.iied.org/sites/default/files/pdfs/migrate/15515IIED.pdf

Chavdarova, T. (2014). Risky businesses? Young people in informal self-employment in Sofia. *International Journal of Urban and Regional Research, 38*(6), 2060–2077. https://doi.org/10.1111/1468-2427.12085

Chen, M. A., & Sinha, S. (2016). Home-based workers and cities. *Environment & Urbanization, 28*(2), 343–358. https://doi.org/10.1177/0956247816649865

Cherecheş, R. M., Ungureanu, M. I., Sandu, P., & Rus, I. A. (2013). Defining informal payments in healthcare: A systematic review. *Health Policy, 110*, 105–114. https://doi.org/10.1016/j.healthpol.2013.01.010

Chrenekova, M., Melichova, K., Marišova, E., & Moroz, S. (2016). Informal employment and quality of life in rural areas of Ukraine. *European Countryside, Sciendo, 8*(2), 135–146.

Colombo, E., Menna, L., & Tireli, P. (2019). Informality and the labor market effects of financial crises. *Word Development, 119*, 1–22. https://doi.org/10.1016/j.worlddev.2019.03.001

Cuevas, S., Mina, C., Barcenas, M., & Rosario, A. (2009). *Informal employment in Indonesia*. ADB Economics Working Paper Series, No. 156, Asian Development Bank (ADB), Manila. Retrieved from https://core.ac.uk/download/pdf/194423782.pdf.

Davidescu, A. (2014). Investigating the impact of unemployment rate on the Romanian shadow economy. A complex approach based on ARDL and SVAR analysis. *Romanian Journal of Economics Forecasting, 17*(4), 109–127.

Davidescu, A., & Dobre, I. (2012). The causal relationship between unemployment rate and U.S shadow economy. A Tado-Yamamoto approach. *Journal of Social and Economic Statistics, 1*(1), 21–34.

Davidescu, A., & Dobre, I. (2013). Revisiting the relationship between shadow economy and the level of unemployment rate: A SVAR empirical investigation for the case of United States. *Journal of Applied Quantitative Methods, 8*(3), 11–19.

De Soto, H. (1989). *The other path – The invisible revolution in the third world*. I.B. Tauris & Co Ltd. Publishers.

Dell'Anno, R., Gomez-Antonio, M., & Alanon Pardo, A. (2007). Shadow economy in three different Mediterranean Countries: France, Spain and Greece. A MIMIC Approach. *Empirical Economics, 33*, 51–84.

Dell'Anno, R., & Solomon, O. H. (2008). Shadow economy and unemployment rate in USA: Is there a structural relationship? An empirical analysis. *Applied Economics, 40*(19), 2537–2555.

Dellot, B. (2012). *Untapped enterprise: Learning to live with the informal economy*. Royal Society of the Arts.

Dike, O. (2019). *Informal employment and work health risks: Evidence from Cambodia*. MPRA Paper No. 92943. Retrieved July 05, 2021, from https://mpra.ub.uni-muenchen.de/92943/1/MPRA_paper_92943.pdf.

Dobre, I., & Alexandru, A. A. (2009). The impact of unemployment rate on the dimension of shadow economy in Spain: A structural equation approach. *European Research Studies, XII*(4), 179–197.

Dohmen, T., Khamis, M., & Lehmann, H. (2010). *Risk attitudes and the incidence of informality among workers: Evidence from a transition country*. ESCIRRU Working Papers 22. German Institute for Economic Research.

du Plessis, V., Beshiri, R., Bollman, R. D., & Clemenson, H. (2002). *Definitions of "rural"*. Retrieved April 02, 2021, from https://ageconsearch.umn.edu/bitstream/28031/1/wp020061.pdf.

Ekici, T., & Besim, M. (2014). A measure of the shadow economy in a small economy: Evidence from household-level expenditure patterns. *Review of Income and Wealth, 62*(1), 1–17. https://doi.org/10.1111/roiw.12138

El-Mahdi, A., Amer, M. (2005). Egypt: growing informality 1990-2003 In Avirgan, T., Bivens, L.J., Gammage, S. *Good Jobs, Bad Jobs, No Jobs: Labor Markets and Informal Work in Egypt, El Salvador, India, Russia, and South Africa*, 31–86, Economic Policy Institute, Washington DC.

Elmurodov, S., Allakuliev, A., Tashmuradov, B., Elmirzaev, S., & Hamdamov, S. (2020). Evaluation of the determinants of shadow economy in selected Central Asian countries. *International Journal of Psychosocial Rehabilitation, 24*(8), 6343–6351.

Enste, D. H. (2015). *The shadow economy in industrial countries*. Retrieved March 14, 2021, from https://wol.iza.org/uploads/articles/127/pdfs/shadow-economy-in-industrial-countries.pdf.

Enste, D. H. (2018). *The shadow economy industrial countries*. Retrieved May 20, 2021, from https://wol.iza.org/articles/shadow-economy-in-industrial-countries/long.

European Commission. (2010). *Europe 2020. A strategy for smart, sustainable and inclusive growth*. Retrieved July 01, 2021, from https://ec.europa.eu/eu2020/pdf/COMPLET%20EN%20BARROSO%20%20%20007%20-%20Europe%202020%20-%20EN%20version.pdf.

Eurostat. (2020). *Quality of life indicators – Measuring quality of life*. Retrieved July 05, 2021, from https://ec.europa.eu/eurostat/statistics-explained/index.php?title=Quality_of_life_indicators_-_measuring_quality_of_life#Framework_for_measuring_quality_of_life.

Eurostat. (2021). *Unemployment statistics*. Retrieved July 01, 2021, from https://ec.europa.eu/eurostat/statistics-explained/index.php?title=Unemployment_statistics#Unemployment_in_the_EU_and_the_euro_area.

Feld, L., & Schneider, F. (2010). Survey on the shadow economy and undeclared earnings in OECD countries. *German Economic Review, 11*(2), 109–149.

Feld, L. P., & Frey, B. S. (2007). Tax compliance as the result of a psychological tax contract: The role of incentives and responsive regulation. *Law and Policy, 29*(1), 102–120.

Fialova, K. (2010). *Labor institutions and their impact on shadow economies in Europe*. Retrieved May 11, 2021, from http://citeseerx.ist.psu.edu/viewdoc/download?doi=10.1.1.1013.8440&rep=rep1&type=pdf.

Fields, G. S. (1990). Labor market modelling and the urban informal sector: Theory and evidence. In D. Turnam, B. Salome, & A. Schwarz (Eds.), *The informal sector revisited*. OECD.

Fiess, N. M., Fugazza, M., & Maloney, W. F. (2010). Informal self-employment and macroeconomic fluctuations. *Journal of Development Economics, 91*(2), 211–226. https://doi.org/10.1016/j.jdeveco.2009.09.009

Forastieri, V. (1999). *Improvement of working conditions and environment in the informal sector through safety and health measures*. Retrieved July 05, 2021, from http://www.ilo.int/wcmsp5/groups/public/%2D%2D-ed_protect/%2D%2D-protrav/%2D%2D-safework/documents/publication/wcms_110306.pdf.

Foscht, T., Ernstreiter, K., Maloles, C., Sinha, I., & Swoboda, B. (2013). Retaining or returning? Some insights for a better understanding of return behaviour. *International Journal of Retail & Distribution Management, 41*(2), 113–134.

Gaal, P., Belli, P. C., McKee, M., & Szócska, M. (2006). Informal payments for health care: Definitions, distinctions, and dilemmas. *Journal of Health Politics, Policy and Law, 31*, 251–293. https://doi.org/10.1215/03616878-31-2-251

Gadsby, L., & Samson, R. (2016). *Strengthening rural Canada. Why place matters in rural communities*. Retrieved April 27, 2021, from https://www.decoda.ca/wp-content/uploads/Strengthening-Rural-Canada_Final.pdf

Gapšys, A., & Eičaitė, O. (2010). Šešėlinės ekonomikos žemės ūkio ir maisto produktų rinkoje įtaka šalies biudžetui [The impact of the shadow economy in the agricultural and food market on the national budget]. *Management Theory and Studies for Rural Business and Infrastructure Development, 20*(1), 15–24.

Gerard, F., & Gonzaga, G. (2018). *Informal labor and the efficiency cost of social programs: Evidence from the Brazilian unemployment insurance program*. NBER Working paper No. 22608 (pp. 1–53). https://doi.org/10.3386/w22608

Gerxhani, K. (2004). The informal sector in developed and less developed countries: A literature survey. *Public Choice, 120*, 267–300.

Gerxhani, K., & Werfhorst, H. G. (2011). The effect of education on informal sector participation in a post-communist country. *European Sociological Review, 29*(3), 464–476. https://doi.org/10.1093/esr/jcr087

Giles, D. E. A., & Tedds, L. M. (2002). *Taxes and the Canadian underground economy*. Canadian Tax paper n.106. Canadian Tax Foundation. Canada: Toronto.

Gonenc, S., & Tanrivermis, H. (2007). Factors affecting informal economy of rural Turkey. *Journal of Applied Sciences, 7*, 3138–3153. https://doi.org/10.3923/jas.2007.3138.3153

Gonzalez-Baltazar, R., Contreras-Estrada, M. I., Leon-Cortes, S. G., Hidalgo-Gonzalez, B. J., & Hidalgo-Santacruz, G. (2019). Quality of labor life in workers of the informal economy in Guadalajara, Mexico. In *Advances in social and occupational ergonomics, Proceedings of the AHFE 2019 International Conference on Social and Occupational Ergonomics, July 24–28, 2019, Washington D.C., USA* (pp. 266–276). https://doi.org/10.1007/978-3-030-20145-6_26

Gottschalk, P., & Gunnesdal, L. (2018). *White-collar crime in the shadow economy*. Lack of Detection, Investigation and Conviction Compared to Social Security Fraud. Retrieved April 17, 2021, from https://library.oapen.org/bitstream/handle/20.500.12657/27864/1002140.pdf?sequence=1.

Grimm, M., van der Hoeven, R., & Lay, J. (2011). *Unlocking potential: Tackling economic, institutional and social constraints of informal entrepreneurship in Sub-Saharan Africa: Main findings and policy conclusions*. Retrieved April 30, 2021, from https://openknowledge.worldbank.org/bitstream/handle/10986/26878/779250WP0P11510IC00Summary00PUBLIC0.pdf?sequence=1&isAllowed=y.

Gunther, I., & Launov, A. (2012). Informal employment in developing countries: Opportunity or last resort? *Journal of Development Economics, 97*(1), 88–98. https://doi.org/10.1016/j.jdeveco.2011.01.001

Habib-Mintz, N. (2009). To what extent can the informal economy concept adequately explain the dynamism of the non-formal sector in developing countries? *Journal of International Business and Economy, 10*(1), 1–19.

Harris, L. C. (2008). Fraudulent return proclivity: An empirical analysis. *Journal of Retailing, 84*(4), 461–476.

Hart, K. (1972). *Employment, income and inequality: A strategy for increasing productive employment in Kenya*. International Labor Organization.

Hasanvand, S., Zarra-Nezhad, M., & Montazer-Hojat, A. H. (2016). The analysis of the effect of unemployment rate on the shadow economy in selected developing countries. *Quarterly Journal of Economic Growth and Development Research, 6*(22), 103–118.

Hassan, H. (2016). Determinants and effects of the informal economy: Bangladesh perspective. *SSRN Electronic Journal, 5*. https://doi.org/10.2139/ssrn.2777694

Heitink, E., Heerkens, Y., & Engels, J. (2017). Informal care, employment and quality of life: Barriers and facilitators to combining informal care and work participation for healthcare professionals. *Work, 58*(2), 215–231. https://doi.org/10.3233/WOR-172607

Helmke, G., & Levitsky, S. (2004). Informal institutions and comparative politics: A research agenda. *Perspectives on Politics, 2*(6), 725–740.

Herwartz, H., Tafenau, E., & Schneider, F. (2013). One share fits all? Regional variations in the extent of the shadow economy in Europe. *Regional Studies, 49*(9), 1575–1587. Retrieved April 16, 2021, from http://www.econ.jku.at/members/Schneider/files/publications/2012/herwartz_tafenau_schneider.pdf

Hjort, K., & Lantz, B. (2012). (R)e-tail borrowing of party dresses: An experimental study. *International Journal of Retail & Distribution Management, 40*(12), 997–1012.

Hope, K. R. (2014). Informal economic activity in Kenya: Benefits and drawbacks. *African Geographical Review, 33*(1), 67–80. https://doi.org/10.1080/19376812.2013.838687

Hsu, J. L., & Shiue, C. W. (2008). Consumers' willingness to pay for non-pirated software. *Journal of Business Ethics, 81*(4), 715–732.

Huang, G., Xue, D., & Wang, B. (2020). Integrating theories on informal economies: An examination of causes of urban informal economies in China. *Sustainability, 12*(7), 2738.

Hubert, M., & Debruyne, M. (2010). Minimum covariance determinant. *Advanced Review, 2*(1), 36–43. https://doi.org/10.1002/wics.61

Hussmanns, R. (2004). *Defining and measuring informal employment*. International Labor Office Working Paper. Retrieved from https://www.ilo.org/public/english/bureau/stat/download/papers/meas.pdf

ILO. (2002). *Decent work and the informal economy*. Retrieved July 09, 2021, from https://www.ilo.org/public/english/standards/relm/ilc/ilc90/pdf/rep-vi.pdf.

ILO. (2003). *Report of the conference. Seventeenth International Conference of Labor Statisticians*. Retrieved June 29, 2021, from https://www.ilo.org/public/english/standards/relm/gb/docs/gb289/pdf/icls-17.pdf.

ILO. (2012). *Statistical update on employment in the informal economy*. Retrieved June 16, 2021, from https://www.ilo.org/wcmsp5/groups/public/%2D%2D-dgreports/%2D%2D-stat/documents/presentation/wcms_182504.pdf.

ILO. (2015). *Employment in the informal economy*. Retrieved June 29, 2021, from https://www.ilo.org/wcmsp5/groups/public/%2D%2D-dgreports/%2D%2D-stat/documents/publication/wcms_422437.pdf.

ILO. (2016). *The informal economy in the Republic of Moldova: A comprehensive review*. Retrieved May 03, 2021, from https://www.ilo.org/wcmsp5/groups/public/%2D%2D-europe/%2D%2D-ro-geneva/%2D%2D-sro-budapest/documents/publication/wcms_457542.pdf.

ILO. (2021). *World employment and social outlook-trends 2021*. Retrieved from https://www.ilo.org/global/research/global-reports/weso/trends2021/lang%2D%2Den/index.htm.

International Institute for Environment and Development. (2019). *Bridging the affordability gap: Towards a financing mechanism for slum upgrading at scale in Nairobi*. Retrieved June 22, 2021, from https://unhabitat.org/sites/default/files/2020/05/financing_mechanism_for_slum_upgrading_at_scale_in_nairobi.pdf.

International Monetary Fund. (2021). *The global informal workforce. Priorities for inclusive growth*. Retrieved June 29, 2021, from https://www.imf.org/en/News/Seminars/Conferences/2021/07/23/the-global-informal-workforce-priorities-for-inclusive-growth.

International Organization for Economic Cooperation and Development. (2021). *Trust in government*. Retrieved from https://www.oecd.org/gov/trust-in-government.htm.

Jaminson, D. T., Breman, J. G., Measham, A. R., Alleyne, G., Claeson, M., Evans, D. B., Jha, P., Mills, A., & Musgrove, P. (Eds.). (2006). *Priorities in health* (pp. 155–177). The World Bank.

Kanbur, R. (2009). *Conceptualizing informality: Regulation and enforcement*. IZA Discussion Paper No. 4186. Retrieved from http://repec.iza.org/dp4186.pdf.

Karabchuk, T.S., Nikitina, M. V. (2011). *The structure and dynamics of informal and occasional employment in Russia* (in Russian: Dinamika i struktura sluchajnoj i neformalnoj zaniatosti v Rossii). Vestnik Rossijskogo Monitoringa Ekonomicheskogo Polozhenija I Zdorovja Naselenija (RLMS-HSE) (pp. 97–109). Higher School of Economics, Moscow.

Kavan, P. S. (2013). Factors impacting on the urban informal sector: Seven country studies including PNG. *International Journal of Economic Policy in Emerging Economies, 6*(3), 211–237. https://doi.org/10.1504/IJEPEE.2013.056931

Kettl, D. F. (2017). *Can governments earn our trust?* Polity Press.

Khamis, M. (2009). *A note on informality in the labor market*. IZA Discussion Paper No. 4676. Retrieved from http://ftp.iza.org/dp4676.pdf.

Kireenko, A., & Nevzorova, E. (2015). Impact of shadow economy on quality of life: Indicators and model selection. *Procedia Economics and Finance, 25*, 559–568. https://doi.org/10.1016/S2212-5671(15)00770-4

Kolm, A. S., & Larsen, B. (2003). *Wages, unemployment, and the underground economy*. Retrieved April 03, 2021, from https://www.ifo.de/DocDL/cesifo1_wp1086.pdf.

Kolm, S., & Larsen, B. (2016). Informal unemployment and education. *IZA Journal of Labor Economics, 5*(1), 1–36. Retrieved from https://izajole.springeropen.com/articles/10.1186/s40172-016-0048-6

Krstic, G., & Radulovic, B. (2015). Shadow economy in the business and entrepreneurial sectors. In G. Krstić & F. Schneider (Eds.), *Formalizing the shadow economy in Serbia policy measures and growth effects* (pp. 77–99). Springer.

Krumplyte, J., & Samulevicius, J. (2010). Complex research on undeclared work: Theoretical aspects and empirical application in Lithuania. *Inzinerine Ekonomika—Engineering Economics, 21*(3), 283–294.

Kumagai, S., & Iorio, F. (2020). *Building trust in government through citizen engagement*. Retrieved from https://openknowledge.worldbank.org/bitstream/handle/10986/33346/Building-Trust-in-Government-through-Citizen-Engagement.pdf?sequence=5.

Kundt, T. C. (2017). *Opportunities and challenges for taxing the informal economy and subnational taxation*. Retrieved March 28, 2021, from https://assets.publishing.service.gov.uk/media/5b3b64a6e5274a6fe8b7048e/Opportunities_and_challenges_for_taxing_the_informal_economy_and_subnational_taxation.pdf.

Kyrtsou, C., & Labys, W. C. (2006). Evidence for chaotic dependence between US inflation and commodity prices. *Journal of Macroeconomics, 28*, 256–266.

La Porta, R., & Shleifer, A. (2014). Informality and development. *Journal of Economic Perspectives, 28*(3), 109–126.

Lambert, F., Pescatori, A., & Toscani, F. (2020). *Labor market informality and the business cycle*. IFM Working Paper No. WP/20/256. Retrieved from https://www.elibrary.imf.org/view/journals/001/2020/256/article-A001-en.xml.

Leal-Ordonez, J. C. (2013). *Tax collection, the informal sector, and productivity*. Research Paper No. 2013-22, Banco de México, Ciudad de México.

Lehmann, F., & Terrell, K. (2005). The puzzle of self-employment: New evidence from the Czech Republic. In *Paper presented at seminar at Faculdade de Ciências Ecónomicas e Empresariais*. Universidade Católica Portuguesa.

Lehmann, H., & Pignatti, N. (2018). Informal employment relationships and the labor market: Is there segmentation in Ukraine? *Journal of Comparative Economics, 46*(3), 838–857. https://doi.org/10.1016/j.jce.2018.07.011

Lesnik, T., Kracun, D., & Jagric, T. (2014). Recession and tax compliance – The case of Slovenia. *Engineering Economics, 25*(2), 130–140.

Leyva, G., & Urrutia, C. (2020). Informality, labor regulation, and the business cycle. *Journal of International Economics, 126*, 103340. https://doi.org/10.1016/j.jinteco.2020.103340

Li, Z., Li, J., & He, B. (2018). Does foreign direct investment enhance or inhibit regional innovation efficiency? Evidence from China. *Chinese Management Studies, 12*(1), 35–55. https://doi.org/10.1108/CMS-02-2017-0034

Lithuanian Free Market Institute. (2015). *Shadow economies in the Baltic Sea region 2015*. Retrieved April 14, 2021, from https://www.llri.lt/wp-content/uploads/2015/11/Shadow-Economies-in-a-Baltic-Sea-Region.pdf.

Lithuanian Free Market Institute. (2019). *Reducing shadow economies from drivers to policies*. Retrieved April 12, 2021, from https://en.llri.lt/wp-content/uploads/2019/09/Seseline-ekonomika-EN-internetui.pdf.

Liu, H., Chen, Y., & Long, H. (2011). Regional diversity of peasant household response to new countryside construction based on field survey in Eastern costal China. *Journal of Geographical Sciences, 21*(5), 869–881.

Loayza, N., Oviedo, A. M., Servén, L. (2006). The impact of regulation on growth and informality: Cross-country evidence. In *Unlocking human potential: Linking the informal and formal sectors*. EDGI-WIDER.

Loayza, N. V. (2016). Informality in the process of development and growth. *The World Economy, 39*(12), 1856–1916.

Lopez-Ruiz, M., Artazcoz, L., Martinez, J. M., Rojas, M., & Benavides, F. G. (2015). Informal employment and health status in Central America. *BMC Public Health, 15*(698), 1–12. https://doi.org/10.1186/s12889-015-2030-9

Mabakeng, M. R. (2020). Poor land administration the leading cause for informal land markets in informal settlements. Project: *Using crowd sourced data in monitoring informal settlement upgrading*. Retrieved from https://www.researchgate.net/publication/350192169_Poor_land_administration_the_leading_cause_for_informal_land_markets_in_informal_settlements.

Maftei, L. (2013). A brief analysis of the shadow economy in Europe. CES Working Papers, ISSN 2067-7693. *Alexandru Ioan Cuza University of Iasi, Centre for European Studies, 5*(4), 548–555.

Magidimisha, H. H., & Gordon, S. (2015). Profiling South African gender inequality in informal self-employment. *Journal of Gender Studies, 24*(3), 275–292. https://doi.org/10.1080/09589236.2013.841569

Mahmood, Z. (2020). *Formalizing Pakistan's informal economy policies*. Retrieved April 28, 2021, from https://www.researchgate.net/publication/339068280_Formalizing_Pakistan%27s_Informal_Economy.

Maloney, W. F. (2003). Informal self-employment: Poverty trap or decent alternative? In *Pathways out of poverty* (pp. 65–82). Springer. Retrieved from https://link.springer.com/chapter/10.1007/978-94-010-0009-3_4

Maloney, W. F. (2004). Informality revisited. *World Development, 32*(7), 1159–1178.

Manes, E., Schneider, F., & Tchetchik, A. (2016). *On the boundaries of the shadow economy: An empirical investigation*. IZA Discussion Papers 10067, Institute of Labor Economics (IZA). Retrieved from https://www.econstor.eu/bitstream/10419/145201/1/dp10067.pdf.

Marcelli, E., Williams, C. C., & Joassart, P. (2010). *Informal work in developed nations*. Routledge.

Martinez, L., Short, J. R., & Estrada, D. (2017). The urban informal economy: Street vendors in Cali, Colombia. *Cities, 66*, 34–43. https://doi.org/10.1016/j.cities.2017.03.010

Mauleon, I., & Sarda, J. (2017). Unemployment and the shadow economy. *Applied Economics, 49*(37), 3729–3740. https://doi.org/10.1080/00036846.2016.1267844

Medina, L., & Schneider, F. (2017). *Shadow economies around the world: New results for 158 countries over 1991–2015*. CESifo Research paper No. 6430 America. Retrieved April 02, 2021, from https://papers.ssrn.com/sol3/papers.cfm?abstract_id=2965972.

Medina, L., & Schneider, F. (2018). *Shadow economies around the world: What did we learn over the last 20 years?* IMF Working paper No. WP/18/17 (pp. 2–76).

Minot, N. (2011). *Contract farming in Africa: Opportunities and challenges*. Retrieved March 22, 2021, from https://pdfs.semanticscholar.org/ae75/ead6b671a1cdf47761f8154932dee3ca9cab.pdf.

Mohar, Y., Manjit, S., & Kamal, K. (2007). Relationship between psychological characteristics and entrepreneurial inclination: A case study of students at University Tun Abdul Razak (Unitar). *Journal of Asia Entrepreneurship and Sustainability, III*(2), 1.

Mussurov, A., & Arabsheibani, G. R. (2015). Informal self-employment in Kazakhstan. *IZA Journal of Labor and Development, 4*(1), 1–19. Retrieved May 10, 2020, from https://izajold.springeropen.com/articles/10.1186/s40175-015-0031-9

Nagac, K. (2015). Tax system and informal economy: A cross-country analysis. *Applied Economics, 47*(17), 1775–1787. https://doi.org/10.1080/00036846.2014.1002893

National Planning Commission. (2012). *National Development Plan 2030. Our future – Make it work*. Retrieved May 11, 2021, from https://www.poa.gov.za/news/Documents/NPC%20National%20Development%20Plan%20Vision%202030%20-lo-res.pdf.

Nchor, D. (2021). Shadow economies and tax evasion: The case of the Czech Republic. *Poland and Hungary. Society and Economy, 43*(1), 21–37. https://doi.org/10.1556/204.2020.00029. Retrieved from https://akjournals.com/view/journals/204/43/1/article-p21.xml

Neves, D., Aliber, M., Mogaladi, J., & du Toit, A. (2011). *Self-employment in South Africa's informal sector: Prevalence, prospects and policy*. Retrieved April 14, 2021, from http://repository.uwc.ac.za/xmlui/bitstream/handle/10566/4512/psppd_rr_self_emploment_in_south_africa_prevalence_prospects_policy_2011.pdf?sequence=1&isAllowed=y.

North, D. (1990). *Institutions, institutional change and economic performance*. Cambridge Univesity Press.

Nunnally, J. C., & Bernstein, I. H. (1994). *Psychometric theory* (3rd ed.). McGraw-Hill.

Nygaard, K., & Dreyer, M. (2020). *Countries provide support to workers in the informal economy*. Retrieved May 02, 2021, from https://som.yale.edu/blog/countries-provide-support-to-workers-in-the-informal-economy.

OECD. (2002). *Measuring the non-observed economy*. Organisation for Economic and Co-operation and Development.

OECD. (2008). *Declaring work or staying underground: Informal employment in seven OECD countries*. Retrieved July 02, 2021, from https://www.oecd.org/employment/emp/40843646.pdf.

OECD. (2009). *Competition policy and the informal economy*. Retrieved May 29, 2021, from https://www.oecd.org/daf/competition/44547855.pdf.

OECD. (2011). *Compendium of OECD well-being indicators*. Retrieved July 09, 2021, from https://www.oecd.org/sdd/47917288.pdf

OECD. (2012). *Reducing opportunities for tax non-compliance in the underground economy*. OECD.

OECD. (2019). *Definitions of informal economy, informal sector and informal employment*. Retrieved June 29, 2021, from https://www.oecd-ilibrary.org/docserver/103bf23e-en.pdf?expires=1624967232&id=id&accname=guest&checksum=548EF9A74D1968038D8EC7826F7D821B.

OECD Development Centre. (2019) *Tackling vulnerability in the informal economy*. Retrieved July 02, 2021, from https://www.oecd-ilibrary.org/docserver/939b7bcd-en.pdf?expires=1607792007&id=id&accname=guest&checksum=485DAF507F57D3297A3BD1D32183B440.

Ogbuabor, J. E., & Malaolu, V. A. (2013). Size and causes of the informal sector of the Nigerian economy: Evidence from error correction MIMIC Model. *Journal of Economics and Sustainable Development, 4*(1), 85–103.

Ogunrinola, I. O. (2011). Informal self-employment and poverty alleviation: Empirical evidence from motorcycle taxi riders in Nigeria. *International Journal of Economics and Finance, 3*(2), 176–185. Retrieved from http://eprints.covenantuniversity.edu.ng/522/1/IJEF_9086-31105-1-PB_vol3_no2_2011.pdf

Ojong, N. (2017). Gender, the state, and informal self-employment: Perspectives from the mobile telecommunication industry in Cameroon. *International Journal of Social Economics, 44*(11), 1456–1470. https://doi.org/10.1108/IJSE-03-2016-0095

Oviedo, A. M., Thomas, M. R., & Karakurum-Ozdemir, K. (2009). *Economic informality: Causes, costs and policies—A literature survey*. World Bank, Working paper No 167. Retrieved from https://documents1.worldbank.org/curated/en/567571468331805356/pdf/503600PUB0Box3101OFFICIAL0USE0ONLY1.pdf.

Packard, T., Koettl, J., & Montenegro, C. E. (2012). *In from the shadow: Integrating Europe's informal labor*. The World Bank. Directions in Development: Human Development, 70602. Retrieved from http://documents1.worldbank.org/curated/en/458701468035954123/pdf/706020PUB0EPI0067902B09780821395493.pdf

Perry, G. E., Arias, O. S., Lopez, J. H., Maloney, W. F., & Serven, L. (2006). *Poverty reduction and growth: Virtuous and vicious circles*. Retrieved March 28, 2021, from http://siteresources.worldbank.org/BOLIVIA/Resources/Poverty_Reduction_and_Growth.pdf.

Perry, G. E., Maloney, W. F., Arias, O. S., Fajnzylber, P., Mason, A. D., & Saavedra-Chanduvi, J. (2007). *Informality: Exit and exclusion. World Bank Latin American and Caribbean Studies*. World Bank. © World Bank. https://openknowledge.worldbank.org/handle/10986/6730. License: CC BY 3.0 IGO

Petersen, H. G., Thiesen, U., & Wohlleben, P. (2010). Shadow economy, tax evasion and transfer fraud—Definition, measurement, and data problems. *International Economic Journal, 24*(4), 421–441.

Petkantchin, V. (2013). The tax and regulatory causes of the underground economy. *IEM's Economic Note*. Retrieved April 18, 2021, from https://www.institutmolinari.org/IMG/pdf/note0513c_en.pdf.

Pew Research Centre. (2019). *Americans' solutions for trust-related problems*. Retrieved from https://www.pewresearch.org/politics/2019/07/22/americans-solutions-for-trust-related-problems/.

Pfau-Effinger, B. (2017). Informal employment in the poor European periphery. *International Journal of Sociology and Social Policy, 37*(7/8), 387–399. https://doi.org/10.1108/IJSSP-07-2016-0080

Pichio, A. (2003). *Unpaid work and the economy*. Retrieved April 21, 2021, from https://library.oapen.org/bitstream/id/77fe7c26-7353-43c1-a72f-edf5d34bfdba/1006069.pdf.

Pickhardt, M., & Prinz, A. (2012). Tax evasion and the shadow economy. *Edward Elgar Publishing*. https://doi.org/10.4337/9781781006740

Pocius, A. (2015). Šešėlinės ekonomikos ir neoficialaus užimtumo būklės bei tendencijų įvertinimas Lietuvoje [Evaluation of the shadow economy and informal employment trends in Lithuania]. *Lithuanian Journal of Statistics, 54*(1), 18–32.

Portes, A., Castells, M., & Benton, L. A. (1989). *The informal economy: Studies in advanced and less developed countries*. John Hopkins University Press.

Pourreza, A., Rostaminya, M., Khalilabad, T. H., Maleki, S., & Mosavi, S. A. (2018). The impact of formal and informal employment of women on their quality of life: A study in Tehran. *Health Based Research, 3*(4), 379–388.

Prelipcean, P., Bucaciuc, A., & Baicu, C. S. (2016). Social economy and informal economy. Interactions and effects. *Ecoforum, 5*(2/9), 102–108.

Putninš, T., & Sauka, A. (2015). Measuring the shadow economy using company managers. *Journal of Comparative Economics, 23*(2), 471–490. https://doi.org/10.1016/j.jce.2014.04.001

Putninš, T., Sauka, A., & Davidescu, A. A. (2018). *Shadow economy index for Moldova and Romania 2015–2016*. Stockholm School of Economics in Riga, National Scientific Research Institute for Labor and Social Protection.. https://doi.org/10.2139/ssrn.3171741

Putninš, T. J., & Sauka, A. (2011). Size and determinants of shadow economies in Baltic States. *Baltic Journal of Economics, 11*(2), 5–25. https://doi.org/10.1080/1406099X.2011.10840498

Putzel, L., Cronkleton, P., Larson, A., Pinedo-Vasquez, M., Salaz, O., & Sears, R. (2013). *Peruvian smallholder production and marketing of bolaina (Guazuma crinita), a fast growing Amazonian timber species*. Retrieved March 14, 2021, from https://www.researchgate.net/profile/Robin_Sears/publication/283914604_Peruvian_smallholder_production_and_marketing_of_bolaina_Guazuma_crinita_a_fast-growing_Amazonian_timber_species_Call_for_a_pro-livelihoods_policy_environment/links/564a195508ae127ff9867f06.pdf.

PWC. (2017). *Understanding the unpaid economy*. Retrieved April 21, 2021, from https://www.pwc.com.au/australia-in-transition/publications/understanding-the-unpaid-economy-mar17.pdf.

Ramasamy, M., Dhanapal, D., & Murugesan, P. (2017). Effects of FDI spillover on national productivity: Evidence from panel data analysis using stochastic frontier analysis. *International Journal of Emerging Markets, 12*(3), 427–446. https://doi.org/10.1108/IJoEM-11-2015-0246

Ranganathan, M. (2014). 'Mafias' in the waterscape: Urban informality and everyday public authority in Bangalore. *Water Alternatives, 7*, 89–105.

Rei, G. M. (2018). Interactions between criminal economy and legal economy. *Society & Politics, 10*(10), 1–26.

Reimer, B. (2000). *The informal economy in rural Canada*. Retrieved March 12, 2021, from https://www.researchgate.net/publication/228539278_The_Informal_Economy_in_Rural_Canada.

Reimer, B., & Bollman, R. D. (2009a). Demographic, employment, income, and networks: Differential characteristics of rural populations. *Journal of Agromedicine, 14*(2), 132–141. https://doi.org/10.1080/10599240902845120

Reimer, B., & Bollman, R. D. (2009b). *Understanding rural Canada: Implications for rural development and rural planning policy*. Retrieved April 05, 2021, from http://2018.icrps.org/wp-content/uploads/sites/4/2018/06/Reimer-Bollman-2010-Understanding-Rural-Canada.pdf.

Reimers, O. (2014). Tax evasion and the shadow economy. CESifo DICE Report, ISSN 1613-6373. *Ifo Institut - Leibniz-Institut für Wirtschaftsforschung an der Universität München, München,*

12(4), 61–62. Retrieved from https://www.econstor.eu/bitstream/10419/167192/1/ifo-dice-report-v12-y2014-i4-p61-62.pdf

Remeikiene, R., Gaspareniene, L., & Schneider, F. G. (2018). The definition of digital shadow economy. *Technological and Economic Development of Economy, 24*(2), 696–717. https://doi.org/10.3846/20294913.2016.1266530

Renshaw, J. (2002). *The Indians of the Paraguayan Chaco: Identity and economy*. University of Nebraska Press.

Rogan, M., & Skinner, C. (2017). *The nature of the South African informal sector as reflected in the quarterly labor-force survey, 2008–2014*. Retrieved May 11, 2021, from https://www.redi3x3.org/sites/default/files/Rogan%20%26%20Skinner%202017%20REDI3x3%20Working%20Paper%2028%20Informal%20sector%20in%20SA%20-%20QLFS%20analysis.pdf.

Rojas, M. (2013). The subjective well-being of people in informal employment: Empirical evidence from Mexico. *Evidence-Based HRM, 1*(2), 169–186. https://doi.org/10.1108/EBHRM-04-2013-0006

Rosenbaum, M. S., Kuntze, R., & Wooldridge, B. R. (2011). Understanding unethical retail disposition practice and restraint from the consumer perspective. *Psychology & Marketing, 28*(1), 29–52.

Roussceuv, P. J. (1984). Last median of squares regression. *Journal of the American Statistical Association, 79*, 1047–1061.

Rousseeuw, P., & Van Driessen, K. (1999). A fast algorithm for the minimum covariance determinant estimator. *Technometrics, 41*(3), 212–223. https://doi.org/10.1080/00401706.1999.10485670

Roy, A. (2005). Urban informality: Toward an epistemology of planning. *Journal of the American Planning Association, 71*(2), 147–158.

Ruge, M. (2010). Determinants and size of the shadow economy – A structural equation model. *International Economic Journal, 24*(4), 511–523. https://doi.org/10.1080/10168737.2010.525988

Ruiz, M. E., Vives, A., Martinez-Solanas, E., Julia, M., & Benach, J. (2017). How does informal employment impact population health? Lessons from the Chilean employment conditions survey. *Safety Science, 100*, 1–3. Retrieved from https://isiarticles.com/bundles/Article/pre/pdf/86994.pdf

Rutkowski, J. (2011). *Promoting formal employment in Kazakhstan*. Retrieved May 10, 2021, from http://conference.iza.org/conference_files/InfoETE2011/rutkowski_j1928.pdf.

Saafi, S., Farhat, A., & Mohamed, M. B. H. (2015). Testing the relationships between shadow economy and unemployment: Empirical evidence from linear and nonlinear tests. *Studies of Nonlinear Dynamics and Econometrics, 19*(5), 585–608. https://www.degruyter.com/document/doi/10.1515/snde-2014-0021/html

Sahnoun, M., & Abdennadher, C. (2019). *The nexus between unemployment rate and shadow economy: a comparative analysis of developed and developing countries using a simultaneous-equation model*. Economics Discussion Papers, No. 2019-30, Kiel Institute for the World Economy (IfW), Kiel. Retrieved from https://www.econstor.eu/bitstream/10419/196127/1/166450186X.pdf.

Sahoo, B. K., & Neog, B. J. (2017). Heterogeneity and participation in informal employment among non-cultivator workers in India. *International Review of Applied Economics, 31*(4), 437–467. https://doi.org/10.1080/02692171.2016.1257584

Sandoval, V., Hoberman, G., & Jerath, M. (2019). Urban informality: Global and regional trends. *DRR Faculty Publications, 16*, 1–19. https://core.ac.uk/download/pdf/212913154.pdf

Sauka, A., Schneider, F., & Williams, C. C. (2016). *Entrepreneurship and the shadow economy*. Edward Elgar Publishing.

Schneider, F. (2012). *The shadow economy and work in the shadow: What do we (not) know*? IZA DP No. 6423 [accessed 01 07 2021]. Retrieved from http://ftp.iza.org/dp6423.pdf.

Schneider, F., Buehn, A., & Montenegro, C. (2010). New estimates for the shadow economies all over the world. *International Economic Journal, 24*(4), 443–461.

Schneider, F., & Enste, D. H. (2002). *The shadow economy: An international survey*. Cambridge University Press.

Schneider, F., Raczkowski, K., & Mróz, B. (2015). Shadow economy and tax evasion in the EU. *Journal of Money Laundering Control, 18*(1), 34–51. https://doi.org/10.1108/JMLC-09-2014-0027

Schneider, F., & Williams, C. C. (2013). *The shadow economy*. Retrieved October 04, 2021, from https://iea.org.uk/wp-content/uploads/2016/07/IEA%20Shadow%20Economy%20web%20rev%207.6.13.pdf.

Shapland, J., & Heyes, J. (2017). How close are formal and informal work? *International Journal of Sociology and Social Policy, 37*(7/8), 374–386. https://doi.org/10.1108/IJSSP-06-2016-0071

Simutina, N. L., & Leventov, N. N. (2018). Estimation of the impact of the driving forces of the informal employment on its size in the Russian regions. *Espacios, 39*(14), 1–16. Retrieved from https://www.revistaespacios.com/a18v39n14/18391432.html

Sinyavskaya, O., & Popova, D. (2005). Informal labor markets and the Russian workforce: Strategies for survival. In T. Avirgan et al. (Eds.), *Good jobs, bad jobs, no jobs: Labor markets and informal work in Egypt, El Salvador, India, Russia and South Africa*. Global Policy Network, Economic Policy Institute.

Sirkeci, I., & Magnusdottir, L. B. (2011). Understanding illegal music downloading in the UK: A multi attribute model. *Journal of Research in Interactive Marketing, 5*(1), 90–110.

Slavnic, Z. (2010). Political economy of informalization. *European Societies, 12*(1), 3–23. https://doi.org/10.1080/14616690903042724

Slonimczyk, F. (2014). *Informal employment in emerging and transition economies*. Retrieved May 03, 2021, from https://wol.iza.org/uploads/articles/59/pdfs/informal-employment-in-emerging-and-transition-economies.pdf?v=1.

Smolka, M. O. (2019). *Informality, urban poverty and land market prices*. Retrieved June 22, 2021, from https://www.lincolninst.edu/es/publications/articles/informality-urban-poverty-land-market-prices.

Srija, A., & Shirke, S. A. (2014). *An analysis of the informal labor market in India*. Retrieved May 17, 2021, from https://www.ies.gov.in/pdfs/CII%20EM-october-2014.pdf.

Stanculescu, M. (2005). Working conditions in the informal sector. *South East Europe Review for Labor and Social Affairs, 10*, 79–93.

Statista. (2021). *Youth unemployment rate in EU member states as of January 2021*. Retrieved June 21, 2021, from https://www.statista.com/statistics/266228/youth-unemployment-rate-in-eu-countries/.

Stoevska, V. (2012). *Employment and gender differences in the informal economy*. Retrieved April 27, 2021, from https://unstats.un.org/UNSD/gender/Jordan_Mar2012/Presentations/Panel%201.b/Panel%201.b_1_ILO_informal%20employment%20Jordan%202012.pdf.

Stuart, E., Samman, E., & Hunt, A. (2018). *Informal is the new normal. Improving the lives of workers at risk of being left behind*. Working Paper No. 530. Retrieved from https://cdn.odi.org/media/documents/11993.pdf.

Tafenau, E., Herwartz, H., & Schneider, F. (2010). Regional estimates of the shadow economy in Europe. *International Economic Journal, 24*(4), 629–636. https://doi.org/10.1080/10168737.2010.526010

Taiwo, O. (2013). Employment choice and mobility in multi-sector labor markets: Theoretical model and evidence from Ghana. *International Labor Review, 152*(3–4), 469–492.

Tang, S., & Guo, S. (2017). Formal and informal credit markets and rural credit demand in China. In *International Conference on Industrial Economics System and Industrial Security Engineering (IEIS). 23 October 2017*. https://doi.org/10.1109/IEIS.2017.8078663

Tefera, D., & Delbiso, T. D. (2013). The role of informal sector in alleviating youth unemployment in Hawassa City, Ethiopia. In *Conference: 59th ISI World Statistics Congress, 25–30 August 2013*. Retrieved June 02, 2021, from https://www.researchgate.net/publication/282669991_THE_ROLE_OF_INFORMAL_SECTOR_IN_ALLEVIATING_YOUTH_UNEMPLOYMENT_IN_HAWASSA_CITY_ETHIOPIA.

Temkin, B. (2009). Informal self-employment in developing countries: Entrepreneurship or survivalist strategy? Some implications for public policy. *Analyses of Social Issues and Public Policy, 9*(1), 135–156. https://doi.org/10.1111/j.1530-2415.2009.01174.x

Tokman, V. E. (2011). *Regulations in the informal economy*. Retrieved June 22, 2021, from https://www.wiego.org/sites/default/files/migrated/resources/files/Tokman-Regulations-Inf-Econ.pdf.

Torgler, B., & Schneider, F. (2009). The impact of tax morale and institutional quality on the shadow economy. *Journal of Economic Psychology, 30*(2), 228–245. https://doi.org/10.1016/j.joep.2008.08.004

Truong, V. D. (2018). Tourism, poverty alleviation, and the informal economy: The street vendors of Hanoi, Vietnam. *Tourism Recreation Research, 43*(1), 52–67. https://doi.org/10.1080/02508281.2017.1370568

Ulyssea, G. (2018). Firms, informality, and development: Theory and evidence from Brazil. *American Economic Review, 108*(8), 2015–2047.

Ulyssea, G. (2020). Informality: Causes and consequences for development. *Annual Review of Economics, 12*, 525–546. https://doi.org/10.1146/annurev-economics-082119-121914

United States Department of Agriculture Economic Research Service. (2021). *Rural poverty & well-being*. Retrieved June 22, 2021, from https://www.ers.usda.gov/topics/rural-economy-population/rural-poverty-well-being/.

Vorley, B., del Pozo-Vergnes, E., & Barnett, A. (2012). *Small producer agency in the globalised market. Making choices in a changing world oilseeds*. Retrieved April 02, 2021, from http://www.agencyft.org/wp-content/uploads/2013/05/Small-producer-agency-in-the-globalised-market.pdf.

Vorley, B., Lecoutere, E., Mubiru, S., Lunduka, R., Ubels, J., de Beyssac, B. C., & Ikaaba, D. (2015). *Growing inclusion? Insights from value chain development in Ugandan oilseeds*. Retrieved March 12, 2021, from http://pubs.iied.org/pdfs/16563IIED.pdf.

Weng, X. (2015). *The rural informal economy. Understanding drivers and livelihood impacts in agriculture, timber and mining*. Retrieved May 12, 2021, from http://pubs.iied.org/pdfs/16590IIED.pdf.

WIEGO. (2020). *Occupational groups in the informal economy*. Retrieved July 02, 2021, from https://www.wiego.org/informal-economy/occupational-groups

Williams, C. C. (1996). Informal sector responses to unemployment: An evaluation of the potential of Local Exchange Trading Systems (LETS). *Work, Employment & Society, 10*(2), 341–359. Retrieved from https://www.jstor.org/stable/23746605

Williams, C. C. (2007). Entrepreneurs operating in the informal economy: Necessity or opportunity driven? *Journal of Small Business & Entrepreneurship, 20*(3), 309–319. https://doi.org/10.1080/08276331.2007.10593402

Williams, C. C. (2008). Consumers' motives for buying goods and services on an off-the-books basis. *International Review of Retail, Distribution and Consumer Research, 18*(4), 405–421.

Williams, C. C. (2011). Entrepreneurship, the informal economy and rural communities. *Journal of Enterprising Communities: People and Places in the Global Economy, 5*(2), 145–157. https://doi.org/10.1108/17506201111131578

Williams, C. C. (2017). *Entrepreneurship in the informal sector: An institutional perspective*. Routledge.

Williams, C. C., & Bezeredi, S. (2017). Explaining and tackling the informal economy: A dual informal labor market approach. *Employee Relations, 40*(5), 889–902. https://doi.org/10.1108/ER-04-2017-0085

Williams, C. C., & Horodnic, I. A. (2015a). Evaluating the prevalence of the undeclared economy in Central and Eastern Europe: An institutional asymmetry perspective. *European Journal of Industrial Relations, 21*(4), 389–406. https://doi.org/10.1177/0143831X14568835

Williams, C. C., & Horodnic, I. A. (2015b). Self-employment, the informal economy and the marginalisation thesis. *International Journal of Entrepreneurial Behavior & Research, 21*(2), 224–242. https://doi.org/10.1108/IJEBR-10-2014-0184

Williams, C. C., & Horodnic, I. A. (2016). Evaluating the multifarious motives for acquiring goods and services from the informal sector in Central and Eastern Europe. *Journal of Contemporary Central and Eastern Europe, 24*(3), 321–338.

Williams, C. C., & Horodnic, I. A. (2017). Explaining participation in the undeclared economy in Central and Eastern Europe: A demand-side approach. *Post-Communist Economies, 29*(3), 297–312.

Williams, C. C., & Horodnic, I. A. (2020). *Horizon scanning: Early warning signals of future trends in undeclared work*. European Commission/European Platform Tackling Undeclared Work.

Williams, C. C., Horodnic, I. A., & Windebank, J. (2015). Explaining participation in the informal economy: An institutional incongruence perspective. *International Sociology, 30*(3), 294–313.

Williams, C. C., Horodnic, I. A., & Windebank, J. (2017). Explaining participation in the informal economy: A purchaser perspective. *International Journal of Social Economics, 44*(11), 1421–1436. https://doi.org/10.1108/IJSE-03-2016-0099

Williams, C. C., & Kosta, B. (2020). Explaining the cash-in-hand consumer culture in the European home repairs and renovations sector. *Journal of Financial Management of Property and Construction, 25*(3), 387–405.

Williams, C. C., & Kosta, B. (2021). Why do consumers buy from informal sector suppliers in East-Central Europe? A case study of home repair and renovation services. *Economic Alternatives, 1*, 134–152.

Williams, C. C., & Youssef, Y. (2014). Is informal sector entrepreneurship necessity- or opportunity-driven? Some lessons from urban Brazil. *Research Journal of Business Management, 3*(1), 41–53. https://doi.org/10.5430/bmr.v3n1p41

Williams, C. C., & Youssef, Y. (2015). Theorising entrepreneurship in the informal sector in urban Brazil: A product of exit or exclusion? *Journal of Entrepreneurship, 24*(2), 148–168. https://doi.org/10.1177/0971355715586897

World Bank. (2017). *World Bank Report 2017*. Governance and Law.

Yu, D., Blaauw, D., & Schenck, R. (2020). Waste pickers in informal self-employment: Overworked and on the breadline. *Development Southern Africa, 37*(6), 971–966. https://doi.org/10.1080/0376835X.2020.1770578

Zimmermann, K. F. (2012, November). The precarious new world of "informal jobs". *Harvard Business Review*.

The manufacturer's authorised representative in the EU is Springer Nature Customer Service Centre GmbH, Europaplatz 3, 69115 Heidelberg, Germany. If you have any concerns regarding our products, please contact ProductSafety@springernature.com

Printed and bound by CPI Group (UK) Ltd, Croydon, CR0 4YY
30/09/2026
02225467-0008